LIFE OF SYN

LIFE OF SYN
A story of the digital generation
Ellie Rennie

MONASH University
Publishing

Monash University Publishing
Building 4, Monash University
Clayton, Victoria 3800, Australia
www.publishing.monash.edu

www.publishing.monash.edu/books/syn.html

Design: Les Thomas

Cover image: Wall art by Jason Hatcher

National Library of Australia Cataloguing-in-Publication data
Author: Rennie, Ellie.
Title: Life of SYN : a story of the digital generation / Ellie Rennie.
ISBN: 9781921867064 (pbk.)
ISBN: 978-1-921867-07-1 (web)
Notes: Includes bibliographical references.
Subjects: Student Youth Network; Mass media and youth--Victoria--Melbourne; Local mass media--Victoria--Melbourne.
Dewey Number: 302.23099451

Printed in Australia by Griffin Press an Accredited ISO AS/NZS 14001: 2004 Environmental Management System printer. Griffin Press

The paper this book is printed on is certified by the Programme for the Endorsement of Forest Certification schemes. Griffin Press holds PEFC chain of custody SGS-PEFC/21-31-26. PEFC certified wood and paper products come from environmentally appropriate, socially beneficial and economically viable management of forests.

Contents

Part One

Part Two

Part One

School

'You are listening to sin', said the radio announcer. That was a few years ago now and I remember thinking I must have misheard. The music was also a bit odd, plunging into bad taste and then getting good again. As it turned out I had been listening to SYN, and not 'sin'. SYN, I discovered, is made by people between the ages of 12 and 26. The only playlist is the 'sweet 16': a collection of songs they happen to like that week.

SYN stands for the much-too-serious 'Student Youth Network', which nobody can be bothered saying on-air. The cheekiness of the name is deliberate. Audiences like the station because it possesses a child-like innocence – it has none of that polished, fast paced, ad-ridden hype of commercial radio. If you live in Melbourne you can find SYN on the radio, television and the web. If you search hard you can also find a few old copies of their magazine, *Pecado* (which means 'sin' in Spanish), lying around their inner-city headquarters. The SYNners will be listening to their peer-produced content in their rooms, watching it on television or downloading it onto their iPods to take on the train. Some of them tune in and decide 'I can do better', so they call up and book themselves in for a training program. Others are online building the technologies, or in studios telling the newbies which buttons to press.

For all of the talk of a new communications paradigm there are very few stories of the people who are actually experiencing it. SYN is a very small enterprise where people go to learn about, and become part of, the media. The high dramas of media dynasties, acquisitions and political influence lie pretty far from their reality. The 'radical changes' occurring in the mediascape stem from the somewhat sudden, wide-scale participation of ordinary folk in media production and distribution. And yet, as SYN demonstrates, you still need skills, support and networks if you want your media participation to lead to work, or to make it into broader public debate. It is these stories that now need telling. As Soep and Chávez argue, if we are to understand the so-called digital generation, looking at the various media forms (blogging, podcasting, YouTube etc) that young people perform is not enough. Instead, we need to better 'identify what young people actually learn from these experiences, how they benefit, who is shut out from these activities, and what the media project itself contributes to (or detracts from) the public domain' (Soep & Chávez 2010).

I spent almost two years at The House of SYN. What I witnessed was a coming of age story, not just for those involved, but for the media in general. During my time there, social networking became the most popular use of the internet and traditional media institutions were forced to acknowledge the rise of amateur content. SYN, meanwhile, rethought its approach to the online environment. They killed their print publication, dealt with the introduction of digital broadcasting and taught school teachers about a new kind of literacy. In just two years dozens of careers were launched. The SYN radio audience doubled. And they got told off for swearing.

This book is about the role of non-profit media in the digital age, including the opportunities that non-profit media presents and the pressures it faces. It is also about young people's attempts to make an impact on the world around them, and how they continue to deploy old-fashioned methods, institutional structures and technologies – even in the process of promoting new media endeavours.

(De)generation

'Radio is dead', pronounced Bryce Ives during our first meeting in early 2006. Bryce was the station manager, 22 years of age. He warned me not to think of SYN as a radio station: 'The whole point of SYN is that anyone can get involved and they can do what they like here – they can make any kind of media'.

'So why does SYN need a community radio licence?' I asked, a little sceptical.

'The licence gives the whole thing legitimacy. Having a radio licence makes you a serious enterprise. But radio was just a starting point. We have a licence to make things happen'.

Radio was also Bryce's starting point. He grew up in a three-bedroom brick veneer house in Ballarat – a typical suburban home, which he describes as something like the set from *Neighbours*. At the age of 11 he started listening to the radio in his bedroom. There were only a couple of stations in Ballarat, but when Bryce stumbled across 3BBB on the dial, he found a world that was very different from the life he was used to. In the mid-nineties, Ballarat's community station was one of the best in the country. Bryce listened to obscure punk recordings alongside classical music, comic-book discussions and broadcasts of the local footy match 'which was always made to sound more exciting than it actually was'. The announcers sometimes talked 'banal crap' and made mistakes, but some were exceptionally original. Bryce reworked his stereo into a simple recording system and began making radio programs in his bedroom.

At 13 Bryce got a part in a theatre production ('something about goldmining', he told me). The play toured to Singapore, inflating his interest in the world and his teenage ego: 'I thought I could do anything I wanted'. When he arrived home he settled back into his room and switched on the radio. The announcer was reviewing a film and Bryce didn't agree with him. He tried to call the station to give his opinion, but, being a community station, nobody was answering the phone. So he got on his bike and rode down there.

Bryce took it all in. A tangle of old furniture, posters and equipment filled the studio – it was nothing like his suburban family world. He proceeded through the empty office and confronted the presenter. Within a few moments, Bryce was seated in front of the mike, which just seemed to open up to him, and his media career began in earnest. He started his own program at 3BBB, messing with station policy whenever it got in his way. He also applied for the ABC's *Race Around the Corner* (a youth version of *Race Around the World*) and was accepted.

At 18 he moved to Melbourne and began hosting his own community television program, *Dawn's Crack*. Every day he would walk past the SYN kids, whose studio was nearby. 'Who do these people think they are?' he would say to himself. There was a good-looking chap called Sam, nicknamed Samurai, who strutted around in a tight shirt and beads, fixing things. And at least two girls called Jo, both smart and popular. To Bryce, a young country boy, they all looked somewhat arrogant: 'student radio wannabes'. Moreover, they called it The Station, 'like it was some fucking ranch in the Northern Territory'. It was not until a community broadcasting conference on the Gold Coast, where he was receiving an award for his television program, that Bryce realised SYN's ideas about the media were closely aligned to his own. SYN was part of a new wave of media, run by young people and for young people. It didn't matter that he wasn't a student himself. Bryce knew the value of access and experimentation and so did SYN. Before long, the SYNners would be his closest friends.

Without 3BBB Bryce would probably have devoted his life entirely to theatre. Ballarat community radio introduced him to the possibility of media designed to distribute the otherwise hidden stories, obsessions and knowledge of ordinary people. Bryce knew early on that he didn't want to be in the Australian media in any standard way – he wanted to transform it. In 2004 *The Australian* newspaper wrote that Bryce Ives was the representative for 'a generational shift in how media is being produced and managed'. Maybe the big media were just trying to keep up with the kids, but it sounded good to Bryce at the time. And there was always the theatre if it all fell through.

SYN was awarded a community radio licence in 2002 during a highly competitive licensing round. They commenced full-time, city-wide broadcasts the following year – a big achievement for a group of kids. Attracting volunteers, maintaining financial stability and technically staying on-air is an enduring challenge. That afternoon, Bryce was downplaying it with the whole 'radio is dead' thing and I could see why. He was trying to enforce upon me that this is new media, not old.

For one thing, he claimed to know a working model that that could turn the media (as we knew it) on its head: 'anyone can get involved and they can do what they like'. In the past they would have been considered simply amateur, or possibly educational. But SYN's willingness to have novices at the centre of their production engine is what made them seem 'new' – important even.

That morning when I first met Bryce, I was surprised how non-amateur it all seemed. Outside the small meeting room there were a number of different activities going on. The news journalists were planning their next radio show downstairs and a group of core volunteers – known as the 'executive' – were discussing some serious station business. Although there was something of a club feel to it, in that everyone seemed to be there because they wanted to be, SYN seemed purposeful. I had expected to be entering a 'youth project'. This was different: real work was getting done. The concepts 'student', 'youth' and 'network' – S, Y and N – were all at odds with each other. Disciplined preparation, unruliness and serious profession were occurring all at once.

I took a snapshot of a poster on the wall, which seemed to sum it all up. On that poster, nestled inside an ear, is a foetus, a life about to born through the ear canal. The poster was made when SYN had just received its community radio licence and would bring new life to an old platform. During our talk Bryce had described SYN as 'the child' of Melbourne's community broadcasting scene. The metaphor makes sense and not just because the people at SYN are considerably younger than station volunteers elsewhere. SYN was born into a solid and nurturing environment, with helpful station workers from community radio (3RRR, 3MBS, PBS, 3CR) and community television (C31) willing to share their wisdom. SYN's success is partly due to the advice and nurturing it received from their elders. Like most children, SYN listened to the good advice when they needed it and rebelled against other established methods. The SYNners, as I was to discover, like to do things own way.

An Accidental Biography

I wasn't sent there to write their story. I was sent to evaluate a training program, which was to be run by The Salvation Army in partnership with SYN. 'Youthworx' was designed with all the worthy aspects of youth media in place: it targeted homeless young people, combined social work with creative engagement and had an annoyingly misspelt name. However, the Youthworx project took longer to come together than anticipated. I arrived at SYN in 2006 – two years too early to start my research, as it turned out.

In the meantime I decided to get to know SYN to see what kinds of outcomes the station was producing for those already involved. Despite my being a few years too old (you are supposed to be under 26 to be involved) I was welcomed in, as something like their biographer, and granted access to their discussion forums, meetings and social events.

I went into SYN with only a superficial idea of what to expect. This is where the digital generation spends their time; a group whose reality has been buried in myth and promotion, their freedom and politics constantly glossed over. The SYNners I met are part of this story because they are the ones that imagine the organisation, give it an identity and keep it running. This book, however, is not about individuals, or even a generation, but something they have created. People get involved in SYN for the sake of the group, to achieve something that they couldn't on their own. It is the kind of place where it is easy to make friends as long as you are willing to help out or just be present. You will become enmeshed before you know it, giving up your spare time and hoping your old friends will still be there for you when you've had enough. The organisation takes on the character of the people involved, becoming something else when they move on.

When I arrived in 2006, over 5000 young people had been members of SYN in only a few years of broadcasting. Many of them would have been active volunteers at some point, undergoing training and then working on a radio or television program. Others would have made it into executive volunteer roles, managing its operations, or working on the board, directing station policy. If you add the kids that come through in school groups, either as short half-day trainees or term-long radio announcers, the participation figure is much, much higher. Regular volunteer meetings are held to induct new SYNners into the organisation, often with 50 to 100 people turning up on a school night. Even excluding the school groups, the vast majority of SYN members are under 21.

After a while I began to see SYN, the organisation, as a character. If SYN were a person it would be forever young – a slightly demented, troublesome teen that desperately wants fame and responsibility and somehow manages to fluke the important things. But biographies are also written in order to uncover a truth about the time and a place that they exist in – how important people come together to define an age, a movement or a city. Although the subjects of this biography are hardly experts in their field (and SYN is no elite club), they provide a glimpse into a new era and the strategies required to make something of it.

Media technologies are at the centre of that change. Although the consequences for individuals can be easily overstated, it is hard to deny that the media itself is very different to what it was a decade ago. The new ways of producing and circulating information have fundamentally altered liberal democratic societies. Market structures are being challenged by voluntary, amateur production through blogs, wikis, social networking and collaborative creativity in various guises. Much of that activity is based on loosely affiliated networks and nonmarket strategies. It has resulted in confusion and possibly crisis for traditional media and a deeper questioning of what the media is for.

Cultural theorist, Henry Jenkins, writes that 'the culture industries never really had to confront the existence of this alternative cultural economy base' until now: 'Home movies never threatened Hollywood, as long as they remained in the home' (Jenkins 2006, 136). New media gurus, like law theorist Lawrence Lessig (2001), speak of these changes in terms of innovation and technological advancement. Ideas and technologies are arising out of the non-market-based activities of ordinary people – friendship groups and hobbies – rather than through professionalised industry and private gain.

The missing link in much of the new media commentary is *how* we participate. There are different levels of activity occurring the amateur media sphere: basic content sharing (of photos, music and videos), content creation, crowd sourcing, citizen journalism, open source software development etc. All of these activities inform the way information is circulated and some require skill, making the new media environment much more uneven than blanket statements about 'media democracy' can account for. A handful of media corporations or public service broadcasters no longer have exclusive rights over the media. But how easy is it for someone with no influence, experience, power or networks to make a difference? How does that media participation become transformative for an individual or group?

There is an expectation at SYN that you do not have to remain a novice and that media forms are something that we can all become literate in. SYN knows the complexity of digital literacy – a new literacy involving the ability to write, not just read, the forms and languages of digital media content. The formal education system has hardly begun to address changes in communication; generally it assumes new communication technologies to be dangerous for young people rather than empowering, or even just a fact of life.

Bryce was right; SYN isn't just a radio station. SYN is a strategy to deal with the new media environment. It took some existing structures, such as the community-based association and a radio licence, and combined them with new production techniques and networked cultural practices. Importantly, SYN set out to be a training ground and an institutional habitat with a sizeable audience. Through this poorly funded and only loosely organised institution, young people are planning their response to the hard questions: 'Where does new media participation lead to?' 'Who is it benefiting?' They are working out which structures will advance their capacity to communicate, get educated and compete in an increasingly competitive knowledge-based workforce. Some are even trying to make the world a better place. The educators and policy-makers can't seem to keep up, relying on the private sector to deal with whatever major economic and social consequences digital communication throws up. SYN likes to talk about 'youth empowerment', but that's too grand and ambiguous a term to describe what really happens there. I'd say they are mostly 'making their own luck' in a very fuzzy media world, whilst attempting to stay true to the values of community media so that others may benefit when they have moved on.

School Days

There are different versions of how SYN started. The one that interests me most is the station's school days, before it grew up and became independent. I decided to visit Thornbury High, a large secondary school in the multicultural Northern suburbs. Two teachers, Paul van Eeden and Colin Thompson met me at reception in the late afternoon and guided me through the wide corridors, which would usually be crammed with kids, and into the heart of the school. Van Eeden's energy and middle-aged hippy vibe is the kind that kids must respond well to. Thompson, a former Maths teacher, has a slow drawl and is a self-confessed 'sports jock'. When he starts speaking about the media, however, a deep and ambitious interest is revealed. The two teachers struck me as opposites, brought together by a shared passion and many hours of hard work.

They led me into a large room that had been converted into a television studio, kitted out with studio cameras and blue screens. A smaller room off to the side was filled with computers for video editing. This was the production centre of *Class TV,* a weekly television program screened on C31. The walls were covered with newspaper articles on *Class TV* as well as Thornbury High's first media experiment, Radio 3TD. The radio station was long gone, superseded by television, and by SYN. The two teachers were keen to tell their radio story and how SYN was the demise of everything they had worked so hard to create...

One of Thornbury High's[1] brightest pupils was a kid called Rorie Ryan. With the help of the SRC, Rorie had raised money from the Education Foundation (then known as the Small Change Foundation) and was made the school's Junior Citizen for his efforts. He used the money to buy a mixing desk for the school – then set about creating some noise. Broadcasting on ten speakers,

---

1   Formerly Thornbury Darebin Secondary College.

the Junior Citizen started a radio station that could be heard in the corridors and across the playground. The teaching staff were not at all impressed that their school had been turned into a massive ghetto-blaster. The students loved it. Two years later, Rorie was doing work experience at community radio 3RRR and discovered that he could apply for a Temporary Community Broadcasting Licence, which is something like a test licence. Still only 15 years old, he put together an application with the help of one of the English teacher aides. In 1996, Rorie's final year of school, Thornbury High became a licensed temporary broadcaster.

According to Paul Van Eeden, Rorie 'seemed to have this tremendous power over the school'. The kid had keys to everything. Although most of the teachers refused to supervise the radio station on top of their regular workload, Paul Van Eeden, the facilities manager, was an early riser and didn't mind so much. Listening and observing the early-morning broadcasts, Van Eeden realised that radio production was actually good for the kids. They were learning things, having fun, becoming confident and getting to school really early. Before 3TD, Paul Van Eeden was unhappy in his job and looking for another place to teach at. Van Eeden stayed at Thornbury High because 3TD needed him.

Colin Thompson, the new Maths teacher, had his office across the hall from the radio station. The Year 7s kept knocking on his door looking for help when the big kids kicked them off air. Thompson, or Thommo as he is known, became interested in the station and got involved in the licence application. 'The kids were really enjoying it', he told me, 'and they weren't enjoying my maths class'. Letting kids broadcast could have been a disaster and the teachers knew it. 'We were risk takers', said Thommo. 'If we weren't then SYN would never have happened'.

3TD is a heart-warming story. But as it was being told to me, I felt there was a subtext – a critique of the education system as a whole. If schools had been a satisfying place to work, if teaching had been all that teachers wanted it to be, if students were learning things that would make them interested in the world and able to be part of it, then 3TD would never have existed. The students responded to 3TD with energy, engaging in a way that the school curriculum could not achieve. For the teachers, it provided a new kind of learning; students could express themselves on their own terms, resist conformity and understand the media from the other side. They witnessed the intangible lessons that came with active involvement (learning by doing) and sudden public performance. The structure was simple: mostly the kids just played their favourite top 20 songs, or discussed topics from schoolbooks. These basic activities, however, revealed the humorous, down-to-earth culture of kids from the working-class, 'ethnic' suburbs. Paul and Thommo discovered a newfound passion for teaching. The way they tell it, 3TD was a little beam of sunlight in a system that was otherwise a bore for everyone involved.

That said, 3TD was also a time-consuming project. Getting a temporary licence was the first step in applying for a full-time licence in a highly competitive process. I remember it only as a listener with a sudden, strange amount of choice before me. Fourteen community media groups competed for four licences, broadcasting on temporary licences for short stints and sharing channels. Amongst them were Hitz FM and New-Gen, both representing the youth community, and KISS FM, a dance music station. Both Hitz and KISS had rattled the commercial radio industry with their impressive audience stats and major dance music events while New Gen served a younger audience. There was also Nu Country which claimed a social service role (implying that the hard-up prefer country music over other genres), a Catholic station, a Koori station (3KND), JOY FM (for the gay community), a Muslim station and Laugh Radio (comedy recordings).

3TD found itself alongside six other temporary community broadcasters in its first test transmission. Their frequency, 87.1, was a particularly far-reaching piece of the broadcast spectrum. The shows were being heard down the Mornington Peninsula. Eight other schools joined 3TD, providing programming for the test transmissions. 3TD received calls from listeners all over the place who loved what they were doing.

One afternoon, Paul Van Eeden received a phone call from a young man called Nigel Slater who was running SUB FM, a station based at LaTrobe University. The tertiary stations were realistically thinking that there would be only one youth licence awarded, if any. Nigel suggested that 3TD join forces with a group of four university stations and apply for a full-time licence together. 3TD decided to give it a try. However, when it came to meeting with the tertiary stations, some were hostile to the younger kids, offering them bad timeslots and little input at the board level. After two years of negotiations with the tertiary student radio stations, 3TD and RMIT's SRA decided to form their own station. They agreed to call it Student And Youth Radio, or SAY-FM. A young woman called Jo McCarthy, who would later become SYN's president, came up with a better idea: the Student Youth Network. SYN was born.

Full Time, Full On

The year SYN moved from being a temporary radio broadcaster to a full-time station, a young man called Craig Twitt was President. We met at the pub one afternoon so he could give me his own personal archive from his days at SYN. Like Bryce, Craig had grown up in the country and moved to Melbourne after finishing school. He enrolled in a Commerce degree at Melbourne University but felt alienated from many of the kids in his course: 'You're not into sport and you're not into the More Beer society… SYN had a mix of really interesting and eclectic people that you couldn't find in other places. And SYN parties were excellent'.

When I met him, Craig was working at 3MBS as the volunteer coordinator. 3MBS is one of those community broadcasting stations that received a licence back in the 1970s. But when Craig described it to me as 'one of the oldest stations' he was actually talking about the age of the volunteers. Being a classical music station, they attract a high proportion of retirees. Volunteer turnover means something different at MBS than it does at SYN. At MBS it's not because people are going off to get jobs or move cities – 'in 20 years, 80% of their current volunteers will no longer be in this world', as Craig put it. Craig had gotten used to being the young guy around MBS.

Not so at SYN. He was only 27 when I met him, but that is old by SYN's standards. He still looked the same as he did in the photos from SYN's launch. In fact, Bryce like to point out the eyebrow ring: 'That is so nineties, Twitt', and, 'Are you waiting for it to come back into fashion?' When SYN redesigned their t-shirt, Georgia Webster (the training manager), told me it was to get Craig into some new clothes. But I suspect that the insulting, dry humour that most SYNners employ is something they learnt from Craig Twitt himself.

The large folio that Craig handed me that day was filled with newspaper articles, radio schedules, press passes, SYN condoms and stickers. In amongst the paraphernalia was an A4 Melbourne University tutorial sheet. On one side it had a series of essay questions ('what do you understand by the transparency of monetary policy?'). On the other it had Craig's notes for his radio show, *Melbourne's Bitter*. That week's work involved research for an interview with someone from the student union and compiling a list of album tracks he was planning on playing that week: Bob Dylan, Augie March and Art of Fighting. The essay on monetary policy obviously had to wait.

I also found an old envelope addressed to Craig. On the back, someone from SYN had scrawled: 'stop ripping off our humble radio station and renew your membership! You shame us all'. Craig renewed his membership. In fact, not long after our meeting, Craig left 3MBS and returned to SYN as the Assistant Station Manager. Bryce gave him an email name, 'assmanager' (which Bryce thought was hilarious), and set him up with a desk down in the volunteer area, in amongst the day-to-day administrivia.

Craig didn't seem to mind my being around a lot. When I asked him if I could help him out in the office he showed me how to work the membership database and entrusted me with the banking. As I tried to get my head around the numbers, Craig would be nearby, ploughing through grant applications and strategic plans. One day he forwarded me a bunch of files from the SYN newsletter archives:

'Welcome to the very first SYN-FM newsletter! Okay, well it's not really. We're still SRA-FM. However, we're also something else, the result of the Special General Meeting held on Tuesday June 13 [2000]. Thanks to those members that came, drank some free beer, ate some free pizza, and sat through a couple of hours of careful deliberation and discussion about the station's future. The end result was a unanimous vote in favour of merging with 3TD-FM'.

They settled on having a baby as their mascot, with the tagline of 'spit the dummy' or 'smooth as'.

The old SRA newsletters are a bit arrogant. They had no idea of what was to come or the way in which 3TD would cause them to rethink their whole approach to media. There is a strong sense of interests to protect – an inflated, undergraduate identity – demonstrating that the transition from a university club to an open organisation was not entirely 'smooth as'. During the temporary broadcasts, the two groups initially decided to share the airtime – a fifty-fifty split – whilst maintaining distinct identities. The SRA newsletter consoled its membership 'sure, some of it simply won't be up to the same standard, and some of it will be hard to listen to, but at the end of the day, we'll be greatly increasing our audience, and most importantly, our chances at getting a full-time licence'. According to Craig, SRA was largely appalled by the content being produced by the 3TD kids. SRA might have been just a bunch of uni students compared to the bullies that dominated Australia's mainstream media, but they still protected their turf when the little kids asked to join the club.

The Australian Broadcasting Authority,[2] luckily, were not impressed by the line-in-the-sand-pit approach to air-time and made it clear that the groups had to fully amalgamate if they wanted a shot at the licence. Turning SYN into a cohesive whole meant implementing training and coming up with a programming structure where all shows were subject to an evaluation process that was lax by SRA standards but a completely new thing for 3TD. Paul and Thommo fought against demo tape applications and in favour of younger representation on the board, including a rotating President (one year tertiary, secondary the next). They didn't succeed.

The licence application process was arduous and competitive. Stations were permitted to file comments on each other's applications. SYN pitted itself against the two dance music stations, arguing that you could not represent young people through a single music genre. The dance stations were faddish and would cease to be relevant when the music was no longer new and interesting. SYN would offer diversity by nature of its accessible programming grid. Music tastes could come and go, and the station would always be relevant to what young people were listening to. That was the argument, anyhow.

The Sydney licence round came up first. One of the applicants, FBI, sounded more like 3RRR than SYN but it claimed to represent the youth community. FBI won the Sydney licence, overcoming its own dance music competitor. SYN saw FBI's win as 'a strong

2   In July 2005, the Australian Broadcasting Authority (ABA) and the Australian Communications Authority (ACA) merged to form the Australian Communications and Media Authority, or ACMA.

message that the pillars of community, participation, inclusiveness and transparency are paramount in their final decision'. It was a victory for nightclub knock-backs everywhere.

Paul Van Eeden described the Melbourne ABA hearing as 'almost like a trial'. Wanting to fill the cavernous, grand auditorium of the Melbourne Town Hall with SYN supporters, the teachers decided to bus in school classes. The interrogation lasted for an hour and a half, while the school kids got 'bored silly'. When the hearing was over and the ABA stood up to leave, the girls and boys broke out into thunderous applause. Van Eeden remembers the ABA's mistaken response: 'We heard back that they were really impressed with our kids because they were passionate. But the kids all clapped and cheered because they could finally get out of the place'. Adults, he observed, have a different idea of youth empowerment to kids.

There was genuine surprise and relief when it was announced that SYN won one of the Melbourne citywide licences. Indigenous station 3KND also received a full-time licence, while the gay community's JOY FM was awarded a sub-metro licence for the inner city. SYN had received a lot less publicity than the dance stations and had only been on the scene for a short time. The broadcasting authority then issued a further five youth radio licences around the country, including Edge Radio in Hobart and Groove FM in Perth. Now that SYN's licence was won the difficult business of establishing a radio station commenced. The SRA newsletter put it out there: 'Anyone got a rich uncle?'

The rich uncle turned out to be RMIT University who paid for the transmitter in full. But as SYN evolved, the tertiary identity grew weaker. For one thing, voluntary student unionism was killing campus life. And despite SRA's fears, the school-age kids were often better in front of the mike than their elders. The trick was to keep the station young, accessible and fiercely independent.

School's Out

An anonymous SYNner created a Wikipedia entry for the station, which credited Craig as the brains behind the whole thing. Paul Van Eeden emailed me not long after it went up, wanting to set the record straight:

> Craig had no hand in at least the first two years, had nothing to do with the application and became President just before we got the licence… Virtually nothing on the Wikipedia site is true except the first management team. It shows how easily history is rewritten. The media claims Wikipedia is as accurate as the Britannica. The SYN entry is a joke.

Craig agreed the entry was inaccurate and sent a message out asking for it to be edited. I asked Paul why he didn't make the changes himself and he replied that he couldn't access Wikipedia from his school network. For all their pioneering youth broadcasting endeavours, the teachers were having problems participating in new media from behind school walls.

Today, the SYNners regard Paul and Thommo as two old guys who were instrumental in setting up the station, but who ultimately had to go. From my observation, everyone seemed to get along with the teachers whenever they were in the room. However, in private interviews the relationship between the teachers and SYN is more complex; there is certainly a strong suggestion of disparate interests and cultures. SYN could not have teachers involved or it would cease to be an independent environment. The teachers felt that they were the natural protectors of the high school age kids, who would be subsumed in university business without them.

Van Eeden and Thompson drifted off the SYN board of their own accord. I asked them what they thought of the current model, whereby schools are treated as clients rather than having some kind of ownership over the station. 'I think we got shafted', replied

Thommo. Van Eeden and Thompson's innovation was to bring a new kind of literacy into the school. Once it was established, however, SYN needed to become part of the media system. That move allowed them to demonstrate the importance of digital literacy to those in education, without being subservient to it. In this way, SYN is now able to teach the teachers. These days SYN hosts a range of 'learning events' directed at schools, including factsheets and workshops that help teachers better understand blogging, podcasting, interviewing and editing.

I spent a fair amount of my time at SYN thinking about school. The majority of the organisation's income comes from their schools training programs, which were being carefully redeveloped by Georgia Webster while I was there. Georgia had worked her way up through SYN's volunteer ranks to become one of a handful of paid staff (and yes, like Bryce and Craig, she grew up in the country). I was intrigued by her accounts of media studies at the secondary level. In her opinion, it rarely included production and focused on a critical understanding of media texts designed to discourage media participation. When teachers came into SYN they were amazed at the way their students took to radio – not just the DJ role, but the technical and production side of it, including researching issues to discuss on air. SYN was offering a different way of learning that, in many respects, was the opposite of school. The founder of the Educational Video Centre in New York City, Steve Goodman, observed a similar pattern: 'The failure of schools and after-school programs to address the media as the predominant language of youth today, or to recognize the social and cultural contexts in which students live, has resulted in a profound disconnect' (Goodman 2003, 2). I asked the SYNners if they agreed:

'What was it like being trained at SYN?'

'It's a bit of a sink or swim kind of thing so it was very practical, very hands on', one of them replied. 'You sort of see immediate results from what you're learning. Not that you're learning an idea and then years later you get to put it into practice. It's very much 'here's the button you need to press, you go and press it".

'And how did it compare with school or university?'

Someone else responded, thoughtfully: 'I guess, for me, it was my course'.

Schools have historically taken an antagonistic approach to media studies, inculcating a suspicion of the media within the minds of students. Critical media literacy has been the standard approach, whereby students learn about media stereotypes or news values, usually within an English class. This strand of media studies emerged with the study of radio propaganda in the 1930s. By the late 60s it had begun to focus on television and commercialised culture. Students learnt how to translate the semiotic meanings within images, press biases and the illusion of objectivity. However, by teaching students to 'read' the media, but not to 'write' it, schools have distanced students from the media. Elizabeth Daley, Dean of the School of Cinematic Arts at the University of Southern California, writes that 'These courses... enforce the belief that real education remains in books and that real knowledge is rational and linear. Students are taught to read visual texts in order to defend themselves against the onslaught of visual culture. Second, these courses have been extremely one-sided in the definition of literacy, focusing on a "read only" approach' (Daley 2003, 37).

To learn how to make media, to contribute, young people mostly figure it out for themselves. They manage it through the private sphere – social networking sites and content sharing networks (such as Flickr). As media studies professor, John Hartley, has pointed out, digital literacy investment 'is almost all private, seeking to develop markets rather than citizens' (Hartley 2008). Buckingham believes that the attempt to protect young people from the media is doomed to fail. He writes, 'we now need to pay much closer attention to how we *prepare* children to deal with these experiences; and in doing so, we need to stop defining them simply in terms of what they lack' (Buckingham 2000, 16).

Just as schools have tried to shut out the media, advocates for media-based learning have been critical of the school system. In fact, the media has been proposed as an alternative education system that may one day replace the school. In the early 1970s, a radical philosopher called Ivan Illich posited that a network of tape recorders could be used in place of traditional education. Sharing recorded ideas would result in a network of free expression: 'literate and illiterate alike could record, preserve, disseminate, and repeat their opinions' (Illich 1971, 77). Information would be available at the bidding of the student, accessed by tapping into the network. Learning would therefore be search based and peer-to-peer, as opposed to people in authority telling others what they had to know (Illich 1971).

In some respects, SYN echoes the ideas of this strange and visionary philosopher, who lived with a disfiguring cancerous growth on his face out of contempt for the medical system. The institutionalisation of values, in Illich's opinion, led to social polarisation and psychological impotence. In terms of education, the solution was to develop alternative systems of learning, outside of government control:

> The current search for new educational *funnels* must be reversed into the search for their institutional inverse: educational *webs* which heighten the opportunity for each one to transform each moment of his living into one of learning, sharing and caring. (Illich 1971, xix)

New technologies were central to his vision of information webs which would make free speech, free assembly and a free press 'truly universal and, therefore, fully educational' (76). Illich recognised the importance of information storage, skills exchange and technologies that encourage us to think for ourselves, as opposed to closed technologies that turn us into a 'non-inventive' society. As the technologies of Illich's anarchic imagination have become a reality, his depiction of the media and school as polar opposites has persisted. Support for media-based learning is often seated in suspicion of formal education, or, at best, a belief that schools are failing. In such accounts, the legacy of the factory model of schooling – based on efficiency and order suitable for the industrial era – must be overhauled for the challenges of contemporary society. A recurring theme is the playground or community centre as a place of 'supervised freedom' – a more suitable site for learning and self-development than the classroom (Hunter 1994).

For Tom Bentley, former advisor to the Blair government, Illich was ahead of his time (Bentley 1998). Bentley believes that we should seriously consider prospects for education outside of school, and that students only learn at school because it is the place to which they are confined. School is a difficult and forced path to knowledge and independence. He sees an artificial distinction between knowing and doing, so that students do not feel confident putting what they learn to use when they leave school.

I can see where Bentley is coming from, in that changes in society have made the school system an incomplete preparation for what comes next. The well-rounded, independent student that Bentley proposes will have to be prepared for risk – indeed, chaos: 'The main task of a contemporary education system is to prepare its students for a world in which there is less order, less predictability and more chaos, where old solutions are running up against complex, apparently insurmountable challenges' (Bentley 1998, 177). As with much Third Way British thought, Bentley's book tends to depict difficult social conditions as a big adventure we should embrace. This chaotic environment is where education must occur, using the social, cultural and informational resources out there in the world to develop young people's ability to learn for themselves. 'We must develop young people's capacity to learn *in* society, rather than at one remove from it', he writes (6). Learning will take place in schools but also 'in communities, workplaces and families' (1). Bentley wrote that book back in 1998 when he was still in his early twenties. At the end of his time at the UK's Demos, Bentley moved to Australia and took up a job in the Victorian Premiers Department. He became an advisor to the then Deputy Prime Minister, Julia Gillard. I asked him if 'the place of education in an information society' remains the 'first big question' in his mind. He replied:

> Over the decade since *Learning Beyond the Classroom* was written I've come to believe that out of school learning is even more important - and digital media have made more opportunities to connect and enrich these learning opportunities. Education policies now emphasise family, early years and community learning in various ways and schools are extending their hours and their offers. But there is still huge unfulfilled potential in community and project based learning activities and in connecting them rigorously to young people's longer term development. (Bentley 2007, interview)

SYN is happier in the field of informal learning, where discipline and conformity can't reach it. Self-motivated learning, via the media and practice-based organisations, suits its constituents. SYN also relies on schools to keep them going, 'funnelling' kids into their network – and providing an income base. The 3TD teachers originally envisaged that SYN would attain the educational status of the zoo or the museum: a properly funded school excursion destination, providing an organised learning opportunity outside of the classroom. To some extent this has occurred, with organisations such as City Centre (which gives country kids a city experience) building an afternoon at SYN into their school tours, designed to encourage responsibility and self-development through independent learning practices. SYN is also much more than an excursion, having established partnerships with over 150 schools and community associations. You can hear some of them on the *Schools on Air* radio program (formerly known as *Detention*) on weekdays during the school term.

SYN is also developing a TV training program. The expansion into television training mirrors the development of television programming at SYN over the past two years, and the deeper relationship between SYN and Melbourne's community television station, C31.

Accredited training is not currently provided. It was under consideration, but SYN decided to channel the resources through its schools programs. Many believe that too much emphasis on assessment can be a disincentive to get involved. Volunteers seek experience rather than 'pieces of paper' and SYN doesn't want to overschool kids by turning free time into yet another exam.

As much as SYN likes to promote non-school learning, it has maintained a symbiotic relationship with the education system and even provides professional development to teachers. However, SYN likes to appear arms-length from the schools. Where other youth media enterprises (see Soep and Chávez 2010) attempt a difficult balance between adult educators and self-directed or peer learning within their own walls, SYN is prepared to sacrifice expertise for independence. This is not so much a gesture towards some 'authentic' youth voice as a means to give young people a chance to figure things out for themselves. It also keeps the social life of SYN intact, which keeps young people pouring through the door.

Of course, the issue is not just where we learn – in school or out of school – but what it is we should be learning.

Digital Literacy

Before the Greeks began to use written language, Homer and Hesiod (authors, for what it meant at that time) made reference to The Muses, daughters of Zeus, who sang them ideas, delivering some kind of divine creativity. The sisters represented song, memory and practice, producing the preconditions of artistic expression. In the oral culture of Ancient Greece, stories and concepts were maintained and circulated through singing and poetry, using rhythm and formulas easily retained. The Greek classics have remained compelling as a result, even though the divine and curious character – the poetry of it – was a necessity to ensure that the works were remembered. The advent of the written work therefore created anxiety about the effects of literacy; Plato worried that the artful nature of writing would corrupt the integrity of language.

Two centuries on, The Muse was still around and artists tried to capture her image. By that time, however, she was not only reciting and singing, but reading and writing. Classics professor, Eric A. Havelock, uses the image of the writing Muse to introduce the idea that massive social change occurred with the advent of text. When text came along, so did the Greek invention of philosophy, which turned away from song and towards rationality (Havelock 1988).

Just as The Muse learned to write, so a new kind of literacy is emerging and it is considered especially important to the digital generation. They are people who have grown up with the web and mobile telephones and are on the lookout for new ways of using and consuming information. Their ideas and identities are being propelled across different media for their peers to find, sometimes to be felt by a broader public. Who their Muse is and what she is doing, however, I'm not quite sure. Plato's concerns that the written word could inhibit learning suggest that the full informational value of print was not fully realised in his time. The same could be said for digital literacy.

We can say for sure, however, that the languages and forms of digital media have fundamentally changed the way that knowledge is transferred and retained. The emergence of the term coincides with changes in the media, in particular the shift from consumption as the principal form of engagement, to participation. In order to make the most of this newfound capacity, we need to effectively both 'read and write' in the audio-visual-textual languages of the media.

To speak of digital literacy as simply a skill therefore misses the point. Being digitally literate enables participation in society through a communicative system that is elaborate, widespread and decentralised. The concept of digital literacy suggests that there are both social and economic benefits to be gained from widespread fluency in digital media.

Historians have linked print literacy to the acceleration of industry and national economies and the formation of modern social classes. Just as print literacy is now seen as a social necessity, which cannot be separated from the economic advantages it confers on nations, digital literacy is integral to economic and social advancement in a knowledge economy. The points of contention surrounding digital literacy also have a lot in common with the questions spawned by the advent of reading and writing: whether literacy is attained through public or private means and the role of infrastructure and technology, for instance.

The major social changes that historians have attributed to reading and writing came about only when widespread diffusion was achieved. Before 1500 less than 10% of the population of any European nation was able to write and an even lower percentage was likely to have received formal schooling. By 1900, the adult population of a number of European countries had, almost universally, achieved at least minimal literacy. A substantial portion of those populations had considerably higher levels of literacy.

How did that come about? The Reformation was a major force in the spread of literacy and schooling. The movement aimed to change society by teaching the young, with the goal of religious and moral improvement for all. The printing press and the use of the vernacular were central to the Reformers' strategy and the Catholic Church's counter-attack. Although the printing press, which had been in use for some time, did not determine the Reformation (it is more accurate to say that the press made the Reformation possible), the rise of print brought about a communications revolution. The printed word transformed the way that information was disseminated, inducing standardisation of language, and making data collection and preservation possible. The other important step towards near-universal literacy was the formal institutionalisation of schooling, with political control of education largely in place by 1520 (Vincent 2000, Holme 2004).

The spread of reading and writing competency was not necessarily dictated by government, but may have been influenced by pressure from below. As historian David Mitch writes:

> Some historians of public educational policy have noted that popular attitudes toward education could directly shape public policy when that policy was subject to democratic control. Others have found that popular attitudes towards education could influence the effectiveness of public educational policy. And some historians have even argued that the public provision of schooling had a negligible or negative impact on mass education because it displaced private efforts. (Mitch 1992, xv)

Digital literacy is occurring according to a similarly complex mix of private efforts, popular attitudes and government directive. Whether it should be a national, public concern or a private endeavour remains open for debate. If the history of print literacy is anything to go by, universal digital literacy will probably be achieved through a social movement (perhaps social networks), a technological development (the internet) and some kind of government-led effort – although not necessarily in harmony with each other.

Over time, literacy came to mean more than simply the functional ability to sign one's name or write a shopping list. Literacy is now associated with more elaborate and effective use of language; it is not just being able to read a book, but being able to talk and write about a book. Digital literacy similarly involves more complex issues and abstract problems than simple navigation. Media studies professor, John Hartley, once said that print literacy became widespread when it developed into recognisable, replicable forms – for instance journalism and literature (Hartley 2007, private correspondence). The forms and structures of digital literacy are still evolving. Digital literacy is not something we have arrived at, but an ongoing and incomplete experiment. On discussion lists, in studios and at computer terminals, SYNners conduct a continuous conversation on the best way to create content. The SYNners soon realise that to communicate effectively in the media environment, certain forms, standards and methods are useful. SYN gives them basic skills, but it also allows them to practice and enact a suite of audio, visual and textual content forms.

In their book on Youth Radio – a non-profit independent youth media production house in California – Elisabeth Soep and Vivian Chávez unpick the processes and pedagogies that occur in a youth media environment. Their notion of 'converged literacy' encompasses the educational and ethical challenges that young people face when they become media produces. Part of that learning is understanding how to speak to different audiences and leveraging networks in a strategic way to ensure that your message is heard – sophisticated forms of communication where the backing of a prominent community-based organisation also comes in handy.

The system of digital literacy that SYN is engaged in is unfinished business. The seemingly unstructured, casual environments that the youth media sector has developed are, in many ways, an entirely appropriate response to the growing demands of the creative economy. As it is youth-run, the form of digital literacy that results will be what young people see as necessary, not something imposed on them through curricula and exams. But that doesn't make it bereft of purpose, ambition and alliances. The SYNners are still responding to a public discourse and a way of speaking 'outside' their own peer group.

The old content forms will not necessarily be replaced either. Havelock wrote that 'The word *revolution*, though convenient and fashionable, is one that can mislead if it is used to suggest the clear-cut substitution of one means of communication by another. The Muse never became the discarded mistress of Greece. She learned to write and read while still continuing to sing' (Havelock 1988, 22). Meanwhile, as they go about developing and learning new literacies, the SYNners also continue to broadcast.

Broadcasting

SYN lives in an old terrace building on the edge of the city. Walking into The House of SYN is like walking into a shared student dwelling. The old brick walls have stubbornly withstood an inner city pounding, refusing to give in to the pristine architectural creep of nearby universities. The grimy windows make everything appear old; workspaces are lined with worn carpets and second-hand furniture. A computer area has taken over the living room; a reception is now housed in the front bedroom. It is as if a family of undergraduates has been evicted to make way for something more productive. A narrow staircase leads up to the second floor where two or three staff members have their offices, beside a large teaching area. SYN's walls have been painted with graffiti-style murals: flying television sets, space-men with transmitter heads, lined up like space invaders, and a large bald, foetus-like creature, chewing on a SYN logo. Stencilled beside the creature are the words 'SYN never dies, it is consumed and germinates in the minds and sparks the revolution'.

The stencil on the wall – 'SYN never dies' – is a little misleading. SYN never completely dies but it is forced to deal with constant loss and transition. From the moment they arrive, volunteers know that their time at SYN is limited. SYN's access policies are designed to restrict the amount of time anyone can present a show. Aside from the age restriction, there is a 'two block rule', which gives presenters a maximum of 26 weeks of airtime. It sounds exclusionary but it prevents people from sitting on time-slots and not giving others a chance, as happens at other community radio stations. When they no longer have a slot, broadcasters tend to take on other roles, becoming producers, publicists and online developers. To deal with the programming turnover SYN has to keep training new volunteers to replace the old ones. But they will never get away from the rawness of what they make and do because the organisation is filled with kids who are only just beginning to figure out why they are there.

Damian Cavanagh was SYN's radio manager when I arrived. He also presented a very cool new music program, which I listened to on my afternoons in The House. When Damo, as he was known, reached the arbitrary age barrier of 26 he was forced to give up his time-slot. triple j (the national youth broadcaster) soon gave him a job. He became, ironically perhaps, one of triple j's youngest DJs.

Their habit of booting even their best off air is what distinguishes SYN from any other station. It pushes them into a different business model (based on training rather than sponsorship) and allows volunteers to go far in the organisation in a short period of time.

SYN's access policy has its drawbacks. Certain former-volunteers at SYN remain embittered by the experience of being turned out because of age. Some were treasured and talented content-makers, but didn't make an easy transition into the mainstream media, and didn't necessarily want to be involved with SYN at the governance level. Georgia Webster acknowledges that SYN has yet to properly tackle this transitional phase: 'You have a chat with certain key people… and they don't view SYN favourably because of that transition. It is a kick out for them. It wasn't an actual kick out but it wasn't a celebration either.'

Nevertheless, SYN's access policy ensures that the station remains a dedicated youth licensee. The constant volunteer turnover also means that the culture of the place can never turn stale. Melbourne is a city where community radio and television hosts can attract large, dedicated audiences. SYN attracts large audiences, but it is also full of surprises.

Although community radio has been around since the seventies, the original character of the old stations has remained largely intact. 3CR (which began as 3DR – Draft Resistors) is still committed to community activism and social justice while MBS (a classical music station) is dedicated to fine music and arts. 3RRR and PBS are edgy and music-focused. Melbourne's community television channel, C31, is a kind of curated access channel, governed by station members and program providers. 3RRR is probably SYN's closest relative as it was considered a youth station when it launched. Originally an 'educational licence' (before the community licence existed), 3RRR was housed at RMIT, where SYN now has its studios. These days, 3RRR has a turnover of $1.7 million a year and attracts an older listenership within the alternative scene. A number of the SYNners I met applied to do shows at 3RRR but were put on a long waiting list and so came to SYN instead. 'By and large, it's 100% more accessible, like off the chart' one of them told me. 'If you show commitment, you'll get on air at SYN if that's what you want… there's not a chance in hell they'd put you on air at RRR if you are 16, 17, 18'.

The station they really pay out on, however, is triple j, ABC's national youth station. A few SYNners always stood up for triple j, arguing its importance for people living in country areas in particular. Writer Ben Eltham states that triple j's presence in regional and rural Australia 'continues to define the network at its most socially engaged' (Eltham 2009). But most believe it is full of old people trying to talk to kids. When triple j's metropolitan and regional ratings dipped in 2007, former triple j presenter Michael Tunn wrote that the station 'doesn't know young people and has made little attempt to get to know them. A bunch of aging hippies are trying to guess what young people want and they are obviously getting it very wrong' (Tunn 2007).

A colleague of mine, Chris Wilson, pointed out that SYN's rivalry with triple j is not entirely fair. Stations like SYN came about because triple j had paved the way. The commercial sector had dropped the ball on the youth market, aging as their audiences did ('hits from the 70s, 80s and 90s'). Early educational licensees such as 3RRR and 4ZZZ (Brisbane) had already begun to serve the alternative music scene and were not targeted specifically at young people anymore. Youth radio had to be legislated, resourced and licensed. triple j was therefore important in building a national consciousness around non-commercial youth radio. By the late 1990s, however, young people decided they could run it themselves.

The dilemma of accessibility is one of the core features of the new media environment. How do you maintain an audience and attract income with a ramshackle of content dictated by a group of transient, amateur creators with only minimal training? SYN doesn't find it easy. The programming and access policies are constantly up for review, with executive volunteers wanting to polish productions one day and 'keep it raw' the next. They rely on the abstract concept of 'youth voice' to promote themselves to funding bodies (and justify their licence), yet internally question whether such a thing exists. I found myself in the middle of an ongoing, sophisticated debate around aesthetics, professionalism, audiences and access.

In general, however, SYN has learnt that access and quality are not necessarily incompatible, but that coherent structures for training and scheduling can have a positive impact. There are shows that will appear for a block and never come back. Then there are the 'flagship programs', which remain pretty much the same except for the change of hosts. The breakfast program uses the same presenters each weekday for an entire block to maintain consistency. These loose programming strategies seem to work. Ratings for radio doubled between 2004 and 2006, to a total listenership of 124,000. Meanwhile, triple j's Melbourne audience decreased significantly in the same time period to 216,000.

Bryce sent out a review of SYN's breakfast program, *Get Cereal*, which pretty much summed up the station's appeal. The blogger, Tohm, said that SYN's breakfast program was like 'a schoolyard conversation made public' and he meant it as a compliment. The SYN hosts don't try to promote themselves; they are just 'smart-arse nerds'. In contrast, Tohm thinks that watching an ABC comedy quiz show is 'like going to a poorly attended birthday party of someone you don't like on a night when you'd rather be doing something else and you all gather round and sing happy birthday but in your heart there is no joy, only pity'. In other words, it just seems forced. The blog review was backed up by a larger study, conducted by a group of Griffith University academics, headed by Michael Meadows, which analysed audience responses to community radio. They discovered that 'occasional mistakes on-air make audience members feel like the presenters are "one of them" and they feel they are listening to "conversations with friends"' (Meadows et al. 2007, 28).

As the Griffith University study was the first of its kind in Australia, it is difficult to say whether the conversational appeal of community radio has been enhanced with the rise of amateur content more generally, or whether it has always been a winning factor. Although I am suspicious of the concept of singular, or authentic, youth voice, there is some grounds to conclude that community radio can possess preoccupations, energy and even rapport between presenters, which the mainstream media would struggle to fabricate.

SYN's broadcast content nonetheless still deals with many of the same themes and issues as the mainstream media: popular culture, politics, sport, satire and sex. One of the most popular programs is *Asian Pop Night*, produced by Southeast Asian international students, a neglected youth audience if ever there was one. They receive more online fan posts than any other program. *The Naughty Rude Show* is the flagship sex education program, where inexperience is almost a prerequisite. The 'experts' on this show help their listeners get over the whole teen dating issue, answering questions and arguing amongst themselves.

At the other extreme, *Panorama*, the news and current affairs program, is one of SYN's more polished products. The show aims for a 'youth issues' focus but uses the definition loosely, knowing that many political, economic and environmental concerns affect young and old alike. The team, which changes regularly, were usually the ones having in-depth conversations with each other around The House. As I listened it occurred to me that news consumption is only the second most effective way of knowing what's going on in the world. The first is news production: being responsible for informing others is the best motivation for getting informed yourself.

On school days the radio station has what used to be called *Detention*, which is produced by school groups, usually between the ages of 12 and 16. The show is the least predictable. Often, the conversation will involve fairly day-to-day issues. I watched one high school group in the studio as they read out their scripts, like a stilted school presentation. The topics they had set themselves were parental violence for disciplinary purposes (good, 'as long as it's not motivated by drink or having a bad day') and public vs. private schools ('all you learn is to believe that you are better than everyone else'). *Detention* can also produce SYN's most powerful radio. As the rest of the media flared over clashes between Somali 'gangs' and police, a Somali kid unexpectedly used his time on *Detention* to talk about a racial attack on his cousin.

SYN's television programming, *1700* and *Get Cereal TV*, are broadcast live in the mornings and afternoons. *1700* began its life as SYN TV, which was simulcast on radio (basically radio with pictures) but now looks like a variety and music clip program. SYN TV attracted over 30,000 television viewers during its heyday but I felt that *1700* had a tendency to fall back into mainstream afternoon television banality. *Get Cereal TV* is doing better, and SYN's stable of television programs continues to grow.

The former station manager at C31, Greg Dee, loved the SYNners. He told me he was initially worried at the thought of teenagers taking over his offices and live studio every school day. 'Mate, there hasn't been one incident – nothing stolen – and they are perfectly polite', he said. 'What's up with the youth of today?' (Dee 2007, interview).

The SYNners are not always that polite. The station received a formal complaint in August 2007 from a radio listener who had heard the F word used on air. SYN's policy on swearing is to avoid censorship, but with consideration to its audience and the propensity to cause them alarm, distress or shock. Craig felt that the swearing in this particular instance should be taken in context: 9pm on *Punk and Metal Night*. The complaint sparked a surprising amount of interest amongst the membership in regulatory process and SYN's obligations as a broadcaster. These boring issues were being actively discussed and debated. Although it didn't stop anyone from swearing off air (in fact it sparked a flurry of four letter words), the incident brought to the surface a range of issues around responsibility to an audience, station policy and broadcasting law. A bit of swearing, in this instance, turned out to be a good thing educationally.

They key factor of SYN's broadcasting approach is access. SYN repeats mistakes, causes separation issues for some and makes Australia's National youth broadcaster look old. The outcome can be brilliant or banal, sometimes both at once. The youth 'voice' at SYN can mean serious journalism or even 'retro' music shows, made by kids that just want to emulate rather than innovate. For most the fact that SYN is a youth station means nothing more than a foot in the door, or a chance to try an idea, regardless of age.

A New Kid on the Block

In October 2007 an article in *The Age* alerted SYN to a new competitor. Patterson Lakes Primary School had gone and established its own radio station. Although the Grade 6 hosts were sharing a microphone and broadcasting over a tiny one kilometre radius, 'Patto FM' attracted some high profile guests including Rove McManus and Bert Newton. They even managed to get an interview with the darling of Australian talkback radio at that time, Prime Minister John Howard. Brushing off the interview, 12-year-old Mitchell told *The Age*: 'I didn't really feel nervous… It was like asking a normal person' (Ferraro 2007). Their station became famous when two DJs from Triple M launched a war of the airways against Patto, in which they pretended to compete for guests and steal their ideas: 'Their 10 block radius will be ours!'

For SYN the competition was real, however. 'We don't want any more primary or secondary schools setting up radio stations', wrote Bryce on SYN's web-based discussion forum. 'We want them working through us'. A couple of volunteers told Bryce he was encouraging anti-competitive behaviour and that he should 'pick on someone his own size'. Bryce defended his position:

SYN was awarded a licence to represent young people, to provide training and give them access to an audience larger than a couple of blocks. 'Narrowcasting is a fucking joke; it is like standing on the street corner with a megaphone'. And what he hoped was a final statement: 'SYN is the answer'.

Mary chimed in, saying that SYN is also a community broadcaster and that diversity of the media is part of that ethos. But Patto FM probably spent a lot more money than they needed to. The station cost $12,500 to establish, money they raised through their annual Easter Bonnet Parade raffle and fête. Instead, they could have negotiated an hour a week per term for $600 and broadcast to a large audience. The issue was revealing on two counts. Firstly, it showed that John Howard could be 'like a normal person'. The second matter was SYN's inherent contradiction: SYN pitches itself as diverse and accessible, yet it aims to be the first port-of-call for all young people interested in making media. SYN wants big audiences, a city-wide signal and a website that people from far and wide will visit. If SYN didn't have those qualities it would struggle to provide the same level of experience and learning for its volunteers, maintain a serious public profile, set policy agendas and attract funding. The small, cute endeavours of amateur media, such as Patto FM, are nice feel-good stories for the mainstream media, but SYN is something altogether different, asserting that not-for-profit enterprises can be big and important. Or at least somewhere in the middle.

Defence against the Dark Arts

Over a decade ago, when I was completing my undergraduate degree, a book called *Gangland* was released. It was written by cultural studies academic, Mark Davis, who argued forcefully that young Australians were being left out of public debate. The baby boomers, according to Davis, were controlling the media behind the scenes and in front. Young journalists, critics, artists and intellectuals had little chance of breaking down the walls that the 'experts' of the previous generation had created. Our news, magazines, public talks and literature were being dominated by a small group of elites who set the agenda and argued amongst themselves. The rest of us had no choice but to listen (Davis 1997). I remember borrowing the book off a friend's father, who was part of the baby boomer cultural elite. He didn't want it back but I returned it anyhow and tried to tell him why I thought it was right.

Gangland retains its appeal for young people. In May 2007, Bryce posted a link to a new article by Davis and told everyone to read it. The article argued that young people are still not present in the national debates that circulate through the mainstream press and the same old commentators dominate. In other words, 'the gang is still in town'. Some of the SYNners were inspired and others were insulted that SYN didn't get a mention.

Media groups like SYN were once discussed as 'a platform' for young people – a means for an excluded group to have a voice. When I first encountered SYN I assumed it was designed for that purpose. But the fact is that the SYNners have not experienced exclusion from the public sphere in the same way as my generation (Gen X, that is). An alternative has always been there for the Y kids. And exclusion doesn't mean much when there are other, more exciting, places to be.

SYNners seem to spend a lot of time cruising and contributing to online information networks. With this media they can give their opinion, link up with others that feel the same way or sometimes change information if they know it to be wrong (Wikipedia). Their friends are always present, leaving traces across discussion lists and each others' social networking profiles. While some will seek out anonymity at times, mostly they use these communication channels to express their identity and advertise their tastes. They use MySpace or Facebook to post photos, list their interests, alert others to how they are feeling that day and publicise events or issues.

The television, the record shop and the home telephone line are still part of their lives but they can also get the same services from the computer if they know how. It's not necessarily empowerment, but it is a form of self-expression that has caused a significant degree of societal anxiety.

Davis's argument has been overtaken by new concerns. When it comes to young people and the media, the dominant narrative today is that young people are no longer interested in traditional media, at least not the serious stuff like news and current affairs. Often these observations are negatively framed; we are told that young people have abandoned the public realm for trivial activities such as YouTube and MySpace. Having left the protected sphere of old media, they are doing as they please in what is perceived as a dangerous and unregulated digital world. An entire generation has effectively run away from home. Desertion, not exclusion, now characterises the relationship between young people and the media. We no longer worry that they might feel inadequately represented in public debate. The new concern is not 'let them speak' but 'get them back'.

The media reporting on young people, from the point of view of parents, teachers and policy-makers, seemed removed from what I was experiencing. From where I was standing it looked as though the media was just one part of their lives – and a part they seemed to have significant choice and control over. The ABC's television program, *Difference of Opinion*, screened an episode on Generation Y's media use. Social analyst, David Chalke was worried: 'The dark side of who they're connected to and what they are connected to, in an unsupervised and unmoderated way, we still haven't got to grips with. We, as a society, have yet to learn how to teach, to educate, to skill them to live in this world of anarchy' (Chalke 2007).

Every internet user encounters the web's shady innovations: pop-up pornography, identity theft, convenient gambling, and worse. Chalke did not need to explain what he meant by the 'dark side'. The moral fear is that the internet exposes children to bad things (sin, some might say) before they are able to navigate around it. Chalke's solution to the 'dark side' was schooling and parenting. Either kids need to be taught to act responsibly, to grow up, or we should protect them, maintain their childhood (Chalke 2007).

What we can't do is let them roam a digital world alone, apparently. One concerned American parent, Kathleen McDonnell, wrote a book about it, entitled *Honey, We Lost the Kids*. She writes that 'childhood ain't what it used to be. The traditional schedule of maturity has been tossed out the window' (McDonnell 2006, 11). Conversely, slightly older people are often seen to be avoiding adulthood through their media use. An article in *The Age* identified 17,000 young Victorians as part of a 'lost generation', who were not working or studying. A psychologist claimed that the problem was in part due to 'multi-player online games, file-sharing sites like Facebook, and virtual world Second Life'.

Digital media was also the target of health panics, including child obesity. Computers are considered as bad for young bodies as young minds. Stories of people dying of dehydration whilst playing multi-player online games for days on end began to surface. Meanwhile, Georgia Webster (then SYN's education and training manager), decided that the SYNners needed to get active. She chose netball as SYN's team sport and set about putting together a unisex team. SYN purchased some bibs, and came up with a name: the Unisexicorns. Georgia sent a message to her team: 'start jogging!' It had nothing to do with the youth health panic circulating the mainstream media at the time.

If it's not moral corruption or ill health then criminality is the issue. Kathryn Montgomery founded the Centre for Media Education in the US. As an advocate she witnessed the politicisation of children in the passage of various US media and copyright laws. The Digital Millenium Copyright Act, which reinforced copyright laws in an attempt to deal with piracy, resulted in the record industry turning on its own customers. Teens were sued for filesharing songs, flushed out through the electronic networks that linked them into their schools and universities. Children, Montgomery points out, are cast as criminals in their digital activities at the same time as cyber-safety laws cast them as victims (Montgomery 2007). Sonia Livingston also notes the 'high degree of public attention, speculation and contestation that the particular combination of children, media and social change attracts'. On the one hand, young people are perceived as 'the youthful experts or pioneers leading the way in using the internet', while on the other 'as peculiarly vulnerable to the risks consequent on failing to use it wisely' (2009, 2).

Children and young people are criminals and victims because it is easier to worry about how change will impact on the young than to accept that change happens. The UK's expert on digital literacy, David Buckingham, writes that 'In a climate of growing uncertainty, invoking fears about children provides a powerful means of commanding public attention and support' (Buckingham 2000, 11). The crusade against immorality is fought through child pornography laws. Teen deaths ultimately get tracked back to MySpace pages, depicted as a digital magnet for cyber-bullying, satanic influences or just conversations with strangers (especially if the kid was an Emo).[3]

Between the news stories of how the media is a bad influence on children, I was watching advertisements telling me how good it is for them. A child asks his aging dad what the Great Wall of China was built for. The father, who does not have broadband, makes something up, mumbling about keeping the rabbits out. Broadband is an educational necessity, something to be trusted over useless parents.

---

3   An Emo is the contemporary version of a young Goth, or someone who listens to *emo*tional punk-rock music.

So just as children are invoked in panic-stricken discourses on communication technologies, they are also central protagonists in the roll-out of infrastructure and the push for universal access. 2007 was election year – and the year when the national broadband agenda (which involves a complex range of motives known as the 'knowledge economy') was reduced to the straightforward issue of school infrastructure. Once elected, the Labor government moved quickly to get computers into schools. It would be the first election promise to be put into action. The scheme was soon overshadowed by reports of other problems facing public schools. Students were being taught in dilapidated portable classrooms, which were either too hot or too cold. Massive teacher shortages in every state were forcing unqualified staff into science labs or teaching a language they have never spoken. Computers would be welcome, but they could not solve the major problems of education in Australia. Meanwhile, the debate on educational parity was played out across the globe through the digital divide debate, resulting in the wiring of classrooms and libraries and the establishment of ICT centres in developing countries. As Livingstone reminds us, being preoccupied with the internet's 'impact' on society masks the 'importance of other ongoing changes in society, including those that are shaping the internet itself' (2009, 4).

So what do all these competing rhetorics mean? The changes brought about by digital media are not just an issue for young people. They affect us all. If Buckingham is right, and children are used to advance agendas that apply beyond the domain of children, then what are digital generation discourses actually disguising? Although it could be many things, I think it has to do with changes in the nature of audience generally. Internet theorist Yochai Benkler writes we now see the social environment with 'new eyes' – 'the eyes of someone who could actually inject a thought, a criticism, or a concern into the public sphere' (Benkler 2006, 11). We were kept out of mass media production because it was capital intensive and hence professionalised. Now the internet has enabled people to participate in both the production and distribution of information. The anxiety stems from that shift from consumer or audience to participants. The characterisation of digital media as the death of childhood strikes me as a narrative about people who are apparently not ready, not experienced enough, not knowledgeable enough to be contributors. The audience is no longer 'spoken to' (as children are) but we are learning to speak back. As with unruly teens, the way in which the audience speaks is different to the traditional media. Our language – the comments found in blogs, social networking sites, on video 'tubes' – is colloquial, disruptive, rebellious, experimental and unstructured. The audience has reached its adolescent phase and their guardians (media commentators, government, intellectuals) are uncomfortable.

Furthermore, the media itself is seen to be at a critical point in its development. As we watch the demise of traditional media, quality journalism and straightforward payment for cultural products, we hope that something better might also be around the corner. The new landscape may tip towards what is sensible, mature and ethical. Or it might become even more irresponsible, immoral and criminal than its current underdeveloped form. We are facing a rite of passage but don't yet know what's on the other side.

SYN, however, takes teen media participation out of the private sphere and into the public domain. SYN defies the typical characterisation of young people's media use as a purely personal activity that occurs in the family duplex, at the bedroom desk. Cultural theorists have analysed teen blogs and found them to be the contemporary equivalent of the diary. SYN, on the other hand, offers an audience (not just self-expression), critique (alongside peer-review) and friendship groups (online and off). The problem with the concept of 'the digital generation' is not that it overstates competency or the centrality of digital media in young people's lives. The problem is that the term is often used to imply irresponsibility, to categorise what young people do as dangerous play, not learning or work.

So what happened to the netball team? Ken saw it as a uniting force: 'I think netball is going to be the best thing for SYN this year, as it will give us all someone else to yell abuse at other than ourselves'. A few months later it was not looking too good for the Corns. I summed-up their team discussion thread in my diary:

> Lauren, who has the flu, offers to implement biological warfare by coughing on the opponent. But it goes relatively well. Kent reports back that it was the first game where the other team spent more time lying on the ground than the Corns; a dude tried to concuss G-Fox 'but she walked it off'. But 'ermmm, yes. We lost', Ken says. Nonetheless, they played so hard that one of them overslept and was 2 hours 'fashionably' late for work the next day.

You can't be good at everything.

Youth Apathy

Dylan's 18th birthday was an important event. He just missed out on voting in the state election, but enrolled immediately anyhow, knowing the federal election was just around the corner. 'Welcome to democracy', his father told him on the day. 'Prepare to be disappointed'. Dylan's enrolment was also a precursor to one of the low moments in Australia's representative democratic system: the Howard Government's attempt to exclude around 80,000 young people from the Federal Election.

It was easily done. With a majority in both houses, Howard changed the electoral enrolment deadline. If you had not enrolled by 8pm the day the election was called you were simply not eligible to vote (previously, Australian citizens had seven days after the writ was issued to enrol). First time voters were most likely to be excluded from the ballot box on the day, as they were known to leave enrolment until the last minute. At the 2004 election there were 79,000 additions to the roll in the 7 days after the writ had been issued – and they were mostly people who had turned 18 since the previous election. They were also the age group most likely to vote Greens or ALP. Two major campaigns were launched: GetUp!'s Don't Let Them Stop You From Voting and the triple j/AEC Rock Enrol. Brett Solomon from GetUp! likened the change to 'shutting all the shops 33 days before Christmas' (Doherty 2007).

The post-election analysis of these campaigns was upbeat: The Weekend Australian reported that the number of 18-year-olds eligible to vote jumped by 10.3%, while *The Age* found there were 100,000 more 18–24-year-olds on the roll than in 2004 (Megalogenis 2007; Smiles 2007). Youth apathy was declared unfashionable. However, as blogger Peter Brent deduced, in proportional terms the enrolment increase was only slight for 18-year-olds (Jackman; Brent 2007). As the size of the 18–24-year-old bracket had increased in the population, the rates of enrolment amongst that larger group may have gone backwards slightly. Furthermore, young voters had two days more to enrol than initially expected, only because the writ was issued on a Wednesday, rather than the typical Monday (possibly because the Howard government was trying to dodge some bad press on the enrolment issue). The late writ may have boosted figures by giving young voters two days warning. Nonetheless, a small decline was still a better result than the significant losses that might have occurred without the pre-election campaigns.

In some respects it was harder for a young person to avoid the 2007 election than previous ones. Kevin Rudd's digital headshot pursued young voters across YouTube and Facebook, doing his very best to make Howard look old and irrelevant. Commentators said that satire, not news, was sparking the interest of an apparently otherwise apathetic demographic. But, as Gen Y expert Rebecca Huntley has pointed out, the new signs of youth engagement could not be entirely attributed to The Chaser driving a fake motorcade past security and into the APEC summit (Huntley 2008, 104). A raft of policies had adversely affected young people during the long Howard reign, which stretched back as far as their political memory would take them. Ben Eltham, a former curator of the National Student Media Conference and a founder of the Straight Out of Brisbane Festival, wrote that Work Choices, climate change, education and housing were 'against the interests of young people – generally to the benefit of their elders' (Eltham 2007).

New forms of political activism (such as GetUp!) found their feet just as a new breed of journalist-bloggers, like Eltham, began appearing in online publications such as *New Matilda*[4] and *On Line Opinion*. And it wasn't just occurring in youth media. My uncle, Kevin Rennie, a retired teacher, started a blog called *Labor View from Broome*, and managed to score himself a seat in the tally-room for the big night. Citizen-journalists were making their presence felt. The way I saw it, both Kevins won that night.

While these forms of online participation had an optimistic aura, some commentators were sceptical. Jason Wilson wrote in *New Matilda* about conferences he had attended that focused on the relationship between new media, politics and the public sphere:

> As is so often the case in discussions of the future, the habits of the young were a particular focal point. Many papers I heard in the parallel sessions bought into this logic and tried to fill it out with examples of political bloggers or blogging politicians, campaigns spilling over onto social networking services and online political activism. All of these are significant up to a point, but are they actually changing

---

4 In May 2010, *New Matilda* folded. Editor Marni Cordell said that *New Matilda* had 'run out of money'. Though Cordell didn't rule out the site returning, *New Matilda*'s revenue had dropped sharply since the site abandoned its subscription model in 2007. Cordell said that the end of *New Matilda* was 'in large part due to the sheer difficulty of selling online advertising in the current media environment'. It returned in October 2010.

election results or enlarging political participation, let alone influencing policy outcomes? And what is its relevance across political systems? (Wilson 2008)

Yet something had shifted.

In 2010, GetUp! won an unexpected victory. A few weeks prior to the federal election, the lobby group issued a High Court challenge to the electoral law changes they had so vehemently opposed three years earlier. To the surprise of even GetUp!, the High Court declared the Howard-era laws invalid and the law reverted to its previous form. GetUp! National Director, Simon Sheikh, called the decision 'historic' (Harrison & Arup 2010).

A week after the first High Court decision, GetUp! achieved another victory in a test case that challenged laws relating to online voter enrolment. In the case, the High Court ruled that a 19-year-old woman should be placed on the electoral roll after having used GetUp!'s OzEnrol.com (AAP, 2010). The implications of these decisions on federal elections are uncertain, but Graeme Orr suggests that there could be implications for law reform (Orr 2010a, 2010b). Orr argues that in Australia, unlike in the US, litigation is not commonly used to pursue law reform:

> …GetUp! was founded – on the model of MoveOn.org – to push progressive values through cyberspace and the broader political process. But it has now flexed its muscles as a promoter of test-case litigation, in the mode of organisations like the Brennan Center for Justice in New York. (Orr 2010a)

When David Marr's *Quarterly Essay* on the silence and repression during the Howard era appeared I was only partly convinced. He successfully exposed the layers of institutionalised secrecy; academics, rights campaigners, whistle-blowers, trade unions and journalists were subtly or overtly being silenced (Marr 2007). However, the supposed impact on the public psyche – the self-censorship and fall of traditional protest movements – didn't gel for me. While one public sphere was collapsing, another was taking shape.

The most sensible comment I heard on the youth apathy issue came from Tom Dawkins, founder of youth web-forum *Vibewire*. Some months after the election he told me that he didn't believe in youth apathy anymore. In his opinion, apathy is an issue for everyone, not just youth. 'The benefit of youth media is that it offers a way to engage people at a point in their life when they are not fully set in their beliefs and attitudes'.

Youth media is a device that draws attention to broader issues of participation, representation and activism. It will struggle to achieve the influence of other independent media, let alone mainstream media, but it acts as forum where interested individuals can get organised and create worthwhile interventions. Who knows, maybe they will be less 'disappointed' by democracy as a result.

Not Another Whinge Fest

SYN is part of a larger movement that has occurred in Australia over the last decade. The groups that make up the movement convene once a year in Newcastle, NSW. Marcus Westbury is one of the founders of the *This is Not Art* festival (TINA), a national forum for experimental media, music, young writers and emerging artists. He now lives in Melbourne, working as a freelance journalist, television producer and all over arts industry visionary (his ABC television series *Not Quite Art* was launched at TINA 2007). 'Why did the festival remain in Newcastle?' I asked him. 'Because all the professional people who say you are not grown-up or doing it properly have left town', he replied. 'In Sydney and Melbourne there is a sense that you need to be professional or trained or auditioning for something'.

Bryce encouraged me to attend, saying that it was important if I wanted to understand the youth media phenomenon. And it would be fun. The student media program – a staple for many years – was not in the official TINA line-up for 2007, unfortunately. The impact of Voluntary Student Unionism was taking its toll on many student-based media organisations. Bryce, Jess, Craig and others from SYN were going anyway. You need to be at TINA just to get an idea of what's happening around the country, to network or just party, they told me.

TINA was a blur of intense and sometimes uninformed debate, spoken word performances that could send a chill up your spine, bizarre interruptions to the schedule and lots of Newcastle's ginger ale. It was, without doubt, the most fun I have ever had at an arts festival (although that's not saying much). The last day is reserved for the zine fair. Self-published magazines – hand-drawn, photocopied and stapled together – were sold for a few dollars each or given out for free. Gusts of wind caused the little handmade books to flutter and fly about, while their creators did their best to anchor them down with rocks from the park's flowerbeds. TINA continued, as it always does, to make do with whatever it could get its hands on. At the edge of the zine fair, I was given Marcus's rendition of Australia's youth media and arts phenomenon, how it started and why it is different to what came before.

Marcus had edited the student paper at Newcastle University. When he got kicked out of his course for not attending classes, he and a group of friends started an arts and media collective called Octapod. That led to a job as the internet manager for the *Loud* festival (later renamed *Noise*) – a national youth media festival, funded by the Australia Council. 'Suddenly I was plugged into these national networks', Marcus told me. 'I had a reason to be aware of everything that was going on – student radio, community radio, bits and pieces of online stuff'. The job finished in 1997 when Marcus was only 23. Due to the success of *Loud*, the Australia Council were willing to give him $10,000 to set up an online network for young writers, with a face-to-face weekend for skills sharing. Marcus wasn't particularly interested in the online project – 'that was the lie upon which the festival was funded', he admits. But it was a good pretence to bring 100 people from all over the country together; 'community radio people, zine makers, that DIY [do-it-yourself] community'. The following year, 1999, TINA (as it would eventually be named) grew from 100 people to 1000 without any marketing or even a phone, extending into adjacent communities – people who didn't remotely identify themselves as writers. 'It went gangbusters', said Marcus. He described TINA as a 'devolved structure', made up of lots of different smaller festival programs. 'TINA assumes there is space for most things', he reflected, and suggested that the structure of TINA has to do with the fragmentation of culture more generally. There is no obvious political purpose or an assumption that you have to be the best at what you do to be included. And basically, he 'didn't want to do another whinge-fest-student-politics-thing'.

Two important factors contributed to TINA's success. Firstly, the festival always responded to changes in communication technologies, both in terms of its program topics and in its methods of organisation. Secondly, it brought together activities that were considered illegitimate in any other context – zines, for instance had never previously been treated as serious publications by writers' festival organisers. Marcus says: 'we put together an event that recognised that DIY was more than just vanity or not being grown-up enough to do the real stuff yet. It legitimised an ethos, validated a bunch of things. That's the early history of TINA'.

Tom Dawkins was a regular at TINA. After attending his first festival he established Vibewire, an online forum for young people to express ideas and get involved in creative projects. Vibewire was initially intended as an alternative to a wave of commercial 'youth culture' websites that began appearing in 2000, with names like *Juice*, *Tribe* and *Skate*. Such sites would attract heavy investment only to disappear again a few months later. Tom remembers a typical, traditional magazine media interface telling kids what to wear and listen to. The sites had no invitation for people to contribute and very little politics. 'So for some reason, which I can't entirely remember, we thought we could do it better' Tom told me. The core principle of Vibewire was user-generated content. However, as the term didn't exist back then, he called it 'democratic media', 'meaning it was conversation not broadcast'. Vibewire works on the principle that everything is there to be discussed, everything is contestable and no-one is allowed to dictate how things should be. He added, 'If I had known what was involved I wouldn't have done it'.

During TINA, a friend introduced me to her old flatmate, Rachel O'Reilly, a mysterious woman with a low voice whom I felt compelled to draw information out of. As it turned out, Rachel had first attended TINA in 2000 and organised the National Student Media conference at TINA two years later. She kept playing-down her knowledge of the festival and student media generally, even though she seemed to know everyone and had been an editor of the University of Queensland's *Semper Floreat* newspaper back in her uni days. In the past, student newspaper editors participated in TINA, but voluntary student unionism meant that most papers were now strapped for cash. However, she stressed that the relationship between student newspapers and student unions was always fraught, particularly at the older universities where the newspaper team is elected on a separate ticket. 'At *Semper* the back four pages were reserved for union reports, but we put them in small font', she confessed. These days, *Semper* has to raise money from disparate sources to survive, including advertising. The biggest challenge for these publications is still the annual, abrupt changeover of the editorial team and the enduring battles with student political parties. According to Marcus Westbury, student politics is 'not illegitimate but it's puerile and it gets in the way of getting anything done'. Despite their problems, Rachel impressed upon me the deep history of student newspapers and their importance as an independent media. 'Some of the papers go back a hundred years', she said. Urging me to dig deeper, she gave me a list of names and numbers to follow up. 'No-one has done this, but there is a good paper in analysing all of those objects. There is some really great reporting in them, great political analysis. They were a fertile place for a lot of interesting journos to get their writing published. And they are just sitting in a room'. The impact of VSU also needed investigating. Even the folk at TINA had no real idea what was going on, as the current editors were too bogged down in keeping up operations to share information. These artefacts, lying in boxes in some back cupboard of almost every university in the country, were part of the pre-history of SYN. But it was a story that, for now, would have to wait.

I decided instead to track down TIN Radio, Newcastle's youth radio station. The name (This is Not Radio) was an accurate descriptor. Despite being a central pivot for youth arts and culture in Australia, Newcastle has not been able to run a permanent youth radio station. TIN Radio was established by Octapod. The station conducted pirate (unlicensed) broadcasts during the early festivals, moving on to short-term event licences in more recent years. The content was apparently compelling and cutting-edge. For a while, TIN Radio managed to stretch out their broadcasts by applying for pretty much every event they could think of but eventually decided they needed a full-time community radio licence. Unfortunately, ACMA would not issue them with one, on the basis that there wasn't any spectrum available. Since then, TIN Radio has been operating as an online radio station (and broadcasting during the festival) but find it difficult to maintain volunteer interest without a permanent broadcast frequency. Internet radio is just not radio. Not yet, anyhow.

As for Marcus, he developed an ingenious project called Renew Newcastle, which works with property developers to turn vacant or disused buildings into arts spaces for emerging groups until they become commercially viable again. In *Lonely Planet's Best in Travel 2011* guide, Lonely Planet listed Newcastle in its Top 10 cities. Their reason: 'Newcastle now has the most artists per capita nationwide, and the most galleries – from acclaimed regional centres to independent, artist-run spaces and dozens of disused city-centre buildings occupied by photographers, fashion designers, digital artists and more as part of the inner-city regeneration scheme, Renew Newcastle' (Lonely Planet 2010).

Hard Copy

I was handed a copy of *Pecado*, SYN's quarterly magazine, during a presenters meeting, attended by around 50 new SYNners. The issue was small and shiny and each article was set out against a page that had received a designer's attention, careful placement and an editor's scrutiny. The magazine contained articles about bands, interviews, street culture and some short fictional pieces. We all flicked through it quickly and stuffed it into our bags.

Bryce was worried about *Pecado*. As one SYNner commented, it needed to be the kind of publication where people would 'keep back-issues in their cupboards, and their friends always come around and try to steal them, because they don't have those particular issues'. But *Pecado* was not that kind of artefact. Although it was nicely presented and people worked hard to get it to press, SYN's most time-intensive, high-end product was failing to capture the interest of its constituency.

And so Bryce sent a post to the members, which resulted in a discussion thread so long that it made all our eyes hurt. It started with the words: 'My problem is that *Pecado* has become another boring document that SYN is producing that no one really cares about'. *Pecado*, in Bryce's opinion, needed to 'get with the new world and move away from being a traditional A5 magazine'. He suggested it could go online, or become something else entirely. Like a t-shirt or tea towel.

The usual options of e-zines and newsletters were flagged and gathered some support. People began to declare their media consumption habits:

- 'I don't read any magazines at all... I flick through *Pecado*, but don't really 'read' it.

- I prefer to get my media content online (including print, radio and tv... I browse for/download it all).

- The only media I prefer to read in hardcopy is a book.

- Would probably read a tea towel over a zine, simply because it's shorter and is a novelty... but I wouldn't read it four times a year'.

Domesticity won out over digital media, with *Pecado* mugs and pillowcases at the top of the list, adding a whole new dimension to the term 'multiplatform'. Different articles would be sent out in the post to members, designed and packaged to incorporate text somehow. The we-can-do-what-we-like appeal of turning print media into random objects got out of hand. It became known as the 'f*cksh*t installation' proposal.

Pecado was not the only print publication to go under that year. Around the same time it was reported that the world's oldest newspaper had ceased printing and switched to online distribution. Sweden's *Post-och Inrikes Tidningar* was printing only 1000 copies before it went digital but that didn't stop the story from making headlines around the world: it was symbolic of a looming crisis in print media.

I shouldn't really compare *Pecado*'s situation to the panic that hit the print media industry. No serious newspaper gave up their paper edition to produce tea towels, and no journalists lost their livelihood at *Pecado* as they weren't being paid to begin with. The demise of print media spelt the end of a hundred year business model that was seen as integral to the health of the public sphere. The kids at SYN were quick to give their little magazine the boot – possibly too quick. I felt there was some connection. Like many others who publish words on bits of paper, I became a bit fixated with the issue.

Here's the low down: in 1970, over 70% of young Americans were reading the daily newspaper. Now only 35% do. Slightly older readers (such as 30–34 year olds) are turning towards online newspapers (Beecher 2007, 25). Although that is good news for trees, it does not ensure the sustainability of good journalism. Eric Beecher, proprietor of *Crikey*, has pointed out that visitors to online newspapers are worth less than 30% of the value of a print reader (26). Print production costs may be higher, but that is still nowhere near enough revenue to sustain the costs of running a news outlet. In the US, advertising revenue across print and online newspapers was down 23% in 2007 and 2008, and fell a further 26% in 2009. Online revenue for newspapers seemed to plateau around 2007, falling 10% in 2009 after 35% growth rates just a few years earlier. The total revenue of US newspapers fell about 22% in 2009 (Pew Research Center 2010).

Such financial losses have caused many newspapers to close or change hands. The world's most famous news institution, *The Wall Street Journal,* was sold to News Corp. for US$5 billion in May 2007. Large institutions can survive in this way, albeit at a risk to their credibility. Smaller papers don't always have that option of selling out and are unlikely to lure online readers away from brands like *The New York Times* or *The Guardian Online*. Press diversity and independence are the real casualties in the US media. American cities will find themselves without a daily newspaper.

Media critic William Powers writes: 'For all the griping about the institutional constipation of traditional American newspapers – much of it deserved, and a fair proportion of it coming from inside the papers themselves – the fact is, they still produce the vast majority of the journalism that really matters, the ground-breaking work that illuminates the dark places in society and keeps governments honest' (Powers 2006, 57). A former editor of the *Philadelphia Inquirer*, Charles Layton, agrees: 'it's hard to say how newspapers can keep supporting the kind of journalism that sustains a democracy' (Layton 2008). Dedicated, paid journalists knuckling down to quality reporting and investigation are important. The decline in reporting of local council meetings and court hearings – the mundane things that only a paid journalist would sit through – could also have major ramifications for the health of the public sphere.

Here in Australia things are similarly grim. Australian newspaper readerships were in decline even before the advent of online news. Newspaper sales have halved since 1980. Researchers have attributed this phenomenon to information uniformity brought about by ownership consolidation and a reduction in the number of available publications. *The Age* managed to buck trends in 2008 and reported its highest Monday to Friday circulation figures since 1997, possibly the result of discounted subscriptions to schools and universities. Meanwhile, *The Age*'s Chief Executive told his management that the paper expected to see losses of A\$20 million over the next three years.

One SYNner told me that with newspapers available online and next-to-nothing subscriptions for 'students, football club members and god knows what else', he felt he was being ripped off if he had to pay for a newspaper. When his student discount ran out he called *The Age* to find out what other offers he was eligible for. Apparently *The Age Online* was no substitute as it 'privileges superficial lifestyle content' and he can't stand the invasive, flashy ads. He spent an hour and a half one day removing them with an adblock application. This confessed news junkie wants his information to be free and he wants it to be good.

Many of the young people at SYN did care about quality content. Gillian thought that *Pecado* lacked originality, which she attributed to SYN's multiplatform production:

> From the time I joined SYN (a few years ago now), it's basically served to regurgitate what has already been broadcast on the airwaves. I can understand why this is done; I assume it's because SYN aims to be a 'multimedia empire' with all three mediums interlocking and promoting each other. Too much of this 'interlocking', however, means that there is an overwhelming tendency for a generic vision (editorial, aesthetic, or otherwise) to be applied to *Pecado*. Just because it is part of the SYN empire doesn't mean it can't develop its own distinct identity.

Gillian had a point. Overall, the SYNners weren't against the print medium. One *Pecado* volunteer felt that print is more accessible than radio 'because it's permanent'. Such attachment to the physicality and permanency of paper shows that the decline in print readerships amongst young people is a complex issue that may have more to do with content and time than ambivalence to paper. As Powers writes, 'This distinction is not so much generational as operational. The digital medium serves up content differently from paper, and we go to it for different kinds of reading experiences – "search and destroy" versus "settle down"' (Powers 2006, 55).

Besides, other youth organisations were producing successful print publications. One of them is Express Media, with its quarterly magazine *Voiceworks*, which looks something like a creative writing journal. I decided to dig further, curious to know if it was about to turn digital (or into a homewares range). Express Media's former General Manager, Esther Anatolitis, was ironically running Craft Victoria. As I waited to talk to her I perused their gorgeous shop-front - no hippy pottery or macramé in sight, but mugs and tea towels, yes.

'Are young people really apathetic about the print media?' I asked.

'You look at current affairs and the dailies and it is a homogenised product' she said. 'You feel alienated because it's not speaking your language. It is creating this myth that news is all about conflict and controversy, key stakeholders – all those news values'.

'But youth media isn't really alternative media anymore', I responded.

'I agree. Simply pushing the other side of the story is not the answer', she said. In Esther's opinion, to create a real alternative to confrontational media you need to become approachable: 'The challenge for a youth media organisation is to work towards inspiring and engaging people and offering opportunities rather than presenting a front that is exclusivist. A cool kids club is the opposite of what you want to be'.

I pressed her again on the whole print media thing. Isn't it old fashioned? What about the digital generation and all that? Esther, like me, was in her early thirties – not really a digital native – and I wasn't sure if she was speaking for or about youth media. She gave me the run-down on *Voiceworks*: how they turn away scores of stories, articles and poems every issue.

> There is something special for a young person of any age to see their work in print for the first time. There is also something special and unique about a series of magazines that anthologise and become a collection – which you can pick up and look at and keep on the shelf and can share with friends. Facebook doesn't quite replace the tangibleness of the book/magazine or its ability to act as the social interface that you relax with.

Esther was still a mover and shaker in the youth media world and I was to encounter her again some months later at SYN. She reflected the aesthetic, literary and design side of things, which was pretty far from SYN's point of view. Nonetheless, her insights into the value of 'approachable' and 'collectable' media seemed accurate.

Voiceworks survives partly from Australia Council funding. Eric Beecher cites commentators in the US who are calling for philanthropy and state subsidy to maintain the kind of investigative work that appears in publications such as *The New York Times* (Beecher 2007, 26). In the US, not-for-profit organisations like ProPublica and Spot.Us are creating independent, investigative journalism in the name of 'public interest'; the implication being that journalism in the public interest is increasingly scant in the mainstream press. ProPublica and Spot.Us are both are supported by philanthropy, and Spot.Us's funding model focuses on public donations for journalists to investigate stories that are pitched by citizens. Their philosophies are similar: investigative, civic-minded journalism is indispensable in a democracy.

In Australia, the Public Interest Journalism Foundation has launched YouCommNews: a site based partly on the Spot.Us funding model. Its success in Australia remains to be seen. If the industry falls this way, it would not be the first time that private sector has been transferred into the public or third sector domain. As US commentators point out, essential services such as railroads (and now banks) have been handed over to the public when the market has failed to sustain them. 'The suggestion that quality journalism could become charity rather than commerce is a sobering prospect for business that has always been so self-confident in its demeanour and purpose', he writes (26). Sobering for business, but hardly new to those who work in community media.

Interestingly, the magazine where Beecher published his forecasts for the print media, *The Monthly*, reported staggering 83% increase in readership from March 2007 to March 2008, while *The Bulletin* folded. *Crikey*, Beecher's own online subscription news outlet, also experienced significant growth, suggesting that some online models are sustainable, if not hugely profitable. Either Beecher himself is a lucky charm or there is something in the success of these publications that indicates the way forward. At a stab, I'd say readers who do pay for their media are looking for commentary that challenges established opinion rather than reinforcing it.

Pecado was not so lucky. At $14,000 a year, it was too expensive to produce and its distribution too small. Before the year was out, *Pecado* was replaced by an e-zine, which no one wanted to coordinate. The e-zine was then replaced by an e-newsletter that was somewhat thin on content. The *Pecado* volunteers did not get involved but left the e-newsletter to the online team. As Esther had observed, some young writers remain committed to print.

Some months later Macca completed the story:

'Looks like we've had our gun jumped on this one. And they got a better name than "F*cksh*t Installation" too', he wrote on SYN's discussion list. Macca had stumbled across a subscription-based media artefact group, based in San Francisco. Each issue involved a different everyday object that somehow incorporated text, conceived by different artists. *THE THING Quarterly* artefacts included coasters and caps. Although SYN didn't get there first, the definition of print media had finally been torn to shreds.

Part Two

Work

For Australia Day weekend we all headed off to a school camp in Healesville. SYN was holding their Strategic Planning weekend in the complex, which consisted of bunk-rooms, a mess-hall, rope walks and a netball court. On the first evening we watched a debate, or more of an insult-slinging match, on the 'radio is dead' theme. Neither side won or took it particularly seriously. The second night was dedicated to a Karaoke competition, which was taken very seriously indeed. Our days were filled with work; we fought off gigantic beetles and march flies while trying to redesign SYN's programming and training policies. There were lots of people who didn't know anyone and I found myself immersed in conversations about school and work. A 16-year-old girl from the country talked to me about not fitting in at school and getting involved in volunteer work just to ease the boredom. We were looking out at the trees and hills. She described her school camps, where farm kids had to orienteer themselves through Melbourne's CBD. One of their destinations was SYN.

Most of the older SYNners were trying to survive on casual work while figuring out what to do with their lives. Jason Hatcher, a talented graphic designer, was stuck working for a telephone directory. Georgia Ride, the Executive Producer of the news and current affairs program, was confused about her options and not sure how to attain meaningful work. She had just finished her first degree and decided to enrol in a postgraduate journalism diploma. By the time I left SYN Georgia would be working in East Timor, setting up radio stations in villages while Jason had a job in a major sneaker company. The younger SYNners at the camp weren't thinking about their work prospects so much. I had a long conversation with a 17-year-old 'newbie' to SYN about the merits of the Spice Girls, her favourite retro band.

Strategic Planning camp was the moment I refocused my attention from school to work. Aside from their individual anxieties about making the transition into work, it became apparent that SYN itself was a real workplace and an important part of the broader media industries. The planning process was revealing. On the first day, 50 young people listed their 'glads, sads and mads' – the things that made them feel happy, regretful or frustrated about SYN. Under 'glads' they listed opportunities, under-18s getting involved, creative freedom, the new assistant manager, Sweet 16, SYN's forward momentum and podcasting. They were sad about the lack of money, technical failures, volunteer time constraints and the constant loss of skilled people. Selfish people and no digital transmission for Channel 31 were also listed. At the top of the infuriating list was lack of computers for editing, followed by 'dickheads' (people who break equipment, sing over songs and steal CDs). They were also mad about the lack of follow-through on good ideas, not having a receptionist and the public perception that they were only a radio station. Karaoke made it onto all three lists.

Digital Radio

Digital broadcasting was making SYN sad; TIN radio felt the same way. I have to confess that, having followed the issue for some years, I was more mad than sad. The introduction of digital broadcasting was supposed to make spectrum scarcity a thing of the past. Despite the technical capacity to create more channels, in reality, community broadcasters were being squeezed out of radio and television spectrum. We had been told by government that digital transmission would deliver better quality, enhanced broadcasting with greater interactivity and more channels – and that community television would be given a channel to participate. A decade after that promise was made, the sector was still waiting for a channel to start transmitting to the digital television audience. Community television's existing analogue audience base was eroding fast as more people bought digital sets and set top boxes. Meanwhile, the commercial stations had been given large portions of the airwaves – enough for four digital channels each – but at that point they couldn't, or wouldn't, do anything new with it. The folk that had decided to stick with their old analogue box could see that Melbourne's community channel was getting good too. Reviewers began describing it as cult viewing. As the 2013 analogue television switch-off approached, Channel 31 continued to shed audience numbers, and the station's sponsorship revenue declined.

In mid-2009 Greg Dee, C31's station manager of eight years, left the station and became Executive Producer of Arts, Entertainment and Comedy at ABC TV. Dee's successor as station manager, Richard McLelland, was instrumental in building C31's revenue when the station started losing its sponsors. In November 2009, the Federal Minister for Broadband, Communications and the Digital Economy, Stephen Conroy, announced at a community forum that Channel 31 would be allocated broadcast spectrum and given funding to enable digital transmission. After a protracted struggle and over a decade's worth of lobbying and fundraising, Channel 31 was finally transitioning to digital. C31's digital channel – Channel 44 – was launched on 11 June 2010.

However, some have expressed concern about a change in the station's culture since the departure of Greg Dee and the station's digital swithover. A few SYN TV volunteers said that they have felt less welcome at C31. Tahlia Azaria, a SYNner and former C31 staff member, expressed concern that C31 was neglecting its charter: 'I do think that… it's shifting away from what is good for the community and it is moving towards how we can make C31 an equal player in the commercial, digital world' (Azaria 2010, interview).

While C31 made the digital switch, the station was only allocated spectrum that allows them to simulcast their analogue signal with, as yet, no room to develop and program new digital content. The licence was only granted up until switchover, partly due to a scheduled government review into the best use of the 'digital dividend' – the spectrum left over after analogue switch-off – and an impending decision as to whether a fourth commercial licence should be granted. The future therefore still remains unclear for C31.

As for radio, the government decided that the old analogue signal, received by your average transistor radio, should stay. There was no switch-off date as there was for analogue television; digital and analogue would co-exist. Unfortunately, that meant less free spectrum in the long term. Community radio was allocated only 20% of the available capacity on the commercial station's multiplexes (transmission systems) in the cities. Sub-metro stations missed out completely while regional and remote areas would have to wait for their turn at digital. As Melbourne has nine citywide community stations, it was clear to those who bothered to do the math that the 20% allocation would not be enough for each station to simulcast their existing analogue content at FM or superior quality, let alone add-on features such as text or images. At the time, a possible scenario was that the community stations would share airtime and digital broadcasting studios, forming a new, combined digital radio channel.

To me, that sounded like centralisation in a sector that was set-up to be diverse and independent. It seemed that digital community radio would fall through when the sector was unable to reach an agreement with the commercial transmission providers. The new Labor Minister for Communications, Senator Conroy decided to postpone the start-date for digital radio transmission.

It looked like a waste of time and energy for the community broadcasting sector. The peak body, the CBAA, was forced to stay on top of the issues, analyse their position in a changing and somewhat absurd scenario and find resources to devote to a battle they seemed unlikely to win. Craig Twitt attended the appropriate meetings and kept his volunteer army informed of the situation. He implemented a counter-offensive, feeding information to some high profile media journalists who were happy to give Minister Conroy a hard time.

SYN's new President, Jess Crouch, made sure that SYN was seen to be above the whole messy business. She sent a letter to *Crikey*:

> Unless the government pulls a few rabbits out of a few hats and Minister Stephen Conroy starts answering the phone, it seems highly likely that digital radio in Australia will fail. This will mostly be due to the community broadcasting sector's inability to access realistic funding to utilise the technology and convert audiences. But, on the other hand, maybe none of that matters. At my station, a youth community station based in Melbourne, we think the kids have already moved on. There's this other really great broadcasting tool we've stumbled across. It's called the internet. It has moving pictures and everything – and you can get it all on your mobile phone. (Crouch 2008)

There was a question mark over digital radio. There wasn't the same sense of urgency with digital radio as there was with digital television. Many people, like Jess, questioned what digital could offer radio that the internet didn't offer already.

Unexpectedly, digital community radio got off the ground. The Federal Government funded the infrastructure and equipment for community broadcasters. The CBAA appointed a Digital Radio Project Manager – former station manager at Melbourne's 3RRR, Kath Letch – to oversee digital radio distribution for the community radio sector.

Commercial and government stations started broadcasting digitally in 2009, and digital radio for the 37 metropolitan community radio licensees commenced in late 2010. Stations like SYN have the equipment, but spectrum allocation remains a contested issue. Metropolitan community broadcasters share digital multiplexes owned by the commercial broadcasters in each capital city, with community radio services in each city squeezed onto 2/9ths of each multiplex. In Melbourne, all nine full-time metropolitan community broadcasters had to divvy this small amount of spectrum between them. The nine stations, including SYN, were squashed into the same amount of spectrum allocated to four commercial broadcasters and at much lower bitrates. In some capital cities, like Perth and Adelaide, it's an even tighter fit. For many stations, the share is only enough to simulcast an existing analogue signal.

While the take up of digital radio has been slow, the CBAA's Digital Radio Project Manager (now CBAA's General Manager), Kath Letch, emphasised that it is 'stronger than most people in the industry anticipated' (Letch 2010, interview).

The Digital Radio Industry Report states that although digital radio's listener share is only 1.6% compared with analogue radio's 97.2%, that more people are listening to digital radio than are streaming it through the internet. The report also highlights that the take up of digital radio has been highest among those aged 10–17 and 18–24 (Digital Radio Plus 2010).

SYN commenced digital radio broadcasting and digital radio is most popular in its target audience. Up until recently, though, the possibilities of digital had been overshadowed by SYN's concerns about its website.

In 2007, while the community broadcasting sector lobbied for its right to digital spectrum, SYN's online 'discovery' was producing new stresses for the organisation. At the time, digital radio felt like an expensive disaster waiting to happen, but online media also required resources and a strategy. In the broadcast world it was pretty clear that SYN was a youth community station. But what was their identity in the online environment? If Jess was right, the kids were moving on. How could SYN go with them? I was beginning to see cracks in SYN's optimistic outlook.

Don't Be Evil

Towards the end of 2007, Paul Culliver posted a message to the online team:

> Just in case this has gone unnoticed, the SYN.org.au front page is showing: 'Warning: Sablotron error on line 1: XML parser error 3: no element found in /home/website.syn/ main/includes/show_onair_now_pict.php on line 8 XSLT processing error: XML parser error 3: no element found'. Any ideas?
>
> PS. I want a Sablotron for Christmas.

Paul's Sablotron was one of many tiny incidents that amounted to a significant problem. Technology and volunteers don't always work well together, despite media theorists who tell us that technological advancement is fuelled by the goodwill of amateurs. Even in a basic radio studio, things go wrong. The headphones would sometimes fail during an interview and the microphone stand creaked on-air. One Thursday afternoon email from Tahlia warned us all not to touch the broken clock in studio 1: 'Seriously, it's all electrical and shiz. Someone tech-savvy will get onto it eventually...'

When it came to computers, even the tech-savvy people occasionally had to concede defeat. A few of the downstairs computers died long ago, their monitors like tombstones on the grey trestle table. Crashes were common on the working terminals and treated as a kind of omen, especially if caused by the Brontok computer worm, which inhabited The House for months. The SYNners made light of the situation. When it hit there would be a chorus of 'BRONTOKKKKK'DD!' followed by laughter as it wallpapered screens in bright green and pink words of Indonesian hacktivism. Seventeen-year-old Travis set up a Facebook site, 'The Brontok Appreciation Society', where people posted affectionate notes and marvelled at its simple disruptive genius. Georgia Webster wrote on its wall: 'Oh man, when I went to join this group just now, Brontok came up RIGHT AT THE TIME I CLICKED 'join'. It KNEW! Frickin scary'. Hilary composed an ode to the virus, which began with the words 'My deep love of Brontok stretches across eternity and the universe…'

Even without the Sablotrons and Brontoks media convergence is not a seamless evolution. The messy side to it – media companies scrambling for an online presence and facing up to the problems of digital rights management – means that project managers and lawyers are a growing part of the media workforce. At the grassroots end, convergence means consumer-creators pursuing and pushing content across different media, between both the community and commercial spheres. Added to that, there are the issues that are only talked about on the margins of media culture, such as how social movements shift across different spaces and collaborative technological development. From the standpoint of an organisation like SYN, media convergence can also mean a convergence of problems or, at the very least, contrary aspirations knocking up against each other.

That said, nothing was going to stop SYN becoming a convergent media organisation. Their philosophy of allowing people to do what they liked meant that the SYNners would keep venturing into new media territory any way they could.

The easiest way to get in on the multiplatform act was to get a MySpace page, which is exactly what many SYN programmers did. At first, Bryce proposed banning all SYN-related MySpace pages in order to 'protect the integrity of the SYN brand'. Many people agreed that 'MySpace pages look like rubbish anyhow' and that the syn.org.au site should be the primary place for producers to extend their shows. One girl pointed out that SYNners 'should try to refrain from using something like MySpace, which is owned by Murdoch'. However, no-one really knew what to do with that, even if they agreed. Only a few months later SYN had succumbed to social networking's mega peer-group pressure. The prevailing opinion was in favour of using MySpace, or any social networking media, as it would increase the hit-rate for SYN on search engines and enable them to reach more people. Nowadays, syn.org.au gets more hits from Facebook than any other social networking site. Craig Twitt stoically resisted getting a Facebook account but complained that he wasn't getting invited to SYN parties anymore as a result.

An article in *The Australian* newspaper was bugging me: Rupert Murdoch, having purchased MySpace in September 2005 for $US580 million, had stated that 'Community media is undoubtedly the way of the future' (Hopkins 2006). He meant that sourcing and showcasing citizen-made content is the way of the future for large media corporations. But that was just a matter of semantics. Or was it? *Wired* magazine had reported that Murdoch *smiled* as he talked about power shifting from the media elite into the hands of the people (Reiss 2006). That really gave me the creeps.

There was a crisis of sorts occurring and I felt I was one of the few at SYN who could sense it. On the surface, the corporate media were becoming more like community media, or at least displaying a similar appeal due to its participative functions. That posed a series of difficult questions: Should SYN promote the use of commercial media tools? Do ownership and control matter? How could they make a difference in an online environment dominated by the likes of Google and News Corp? If I had articulated those thoughts at the time, I probably would have been shot down immediately. Social networking technologies were well integrated into the culture of this group and there was nothing particularly wrong with that. In fact, it was making publicity, fundraising and recruitment easier. The uncomfortable issue had to do with the role of community media generally. How could SYN, as an organisation, keep its identity in a sea of participatory media choices?

I sat down to map out SYN's distinct qualities. My academic head-voice was telling me that the future of community media rested on definitions. The answers were obvious: community media is essentially very different from user-generated content and social media, even though it is fuelled by similar factors (altruism, social bonds, hobbyist technologies etc). SYN, unlike MySpace, is a community-governed, not-for-profit association. Both are 'user-generated' and provide a means to distribution, but SYN allows for participation in the running of the organisation and the development of technologies. Organisations like SYN are intended to serve identifiable social needs rather than market gaps. They don't use personal information for marketing and tend to consider ethical issues when it comes to advertising. Not-for-profit media does not intentionally restrict the way we access information through technological gate keeping.

The problem with my definition was that it didn't make a lot of difference to the situation at hand. In attempting to 'keep up' with the new media world, SYN wasn't losing any of those qualities. The problem was that it had become a lot harder to differentiate the community media organisation from the corporate user-generated sites. SYN was losing its identity and getting confused as a result, but it had not lost its purpose.

Not-for-profit media doesn't always get things right, but it behaves (or should behave) differently to commercial media simply because it was established for different purposes. In the same way that the methods and aims of charities differ from both government welfare agencies and private companies, community media has its own set of norms and aims (although not necessarily 'charitable' aims). Whilst corporate media may have become participatory, what they then do with our user-generated content needs to be considered and taken in context. Mostly, it is content that they can hook ads onto, or a means to drill into our lifestyle choices and consumption habits for the purposes of market research.

A growing consciousness that the net is not free from control was beginning to emerge amongst commentators. However, little thought had been given to the implications for media ethics. What are the implications of corporate ownership and control online? The issues are certainly different to those of broadcast media. YouTube, as most people know, is now owned by Google, the biggest success story of internet search and advertising. Today, 89% of Australians pour our intentions and desires into Google's search engine. As John Battelle, tech journalist and co-founder of *Wired* magazine, writes in his book *The Search*, the information we provide 'can be discovered, subpoenaed, archived, tracked and exploited for all kinds of ends' (Battelle 2005, 6). The company with the motto 'Don't Be Evil' launched its web browser, Chrome, in September 2008. The original licence agreement included a clause stating that Google would have access to every piece of information a user typed into the browser on any site, with the authority to pass that information on to partner companies. (The licence condition was revoked days after it was released due to public concern.) That's not to say that everything Google does is necessarily evil. In the lead-up to the launch of Chrome, Google was fighting *for* privacy rights in a court battle with Viacom. Viacom had sued Google for $1 billion worth of damages for allowing users to upload clips of their copyrighted material onto YouTube. During the hearing, the judge ordered that Google had to turn over every record of every video watched by YouTube users, as well as their names and IP addresses – a ruling that Google argued went against privacy rights and threatened internet freedom. Commentators have pointed out Google's pioneering spirit when it comes to open source software development. Ryan Paul writes that 'The company is widely recognized as an important ally in the quest to bring software freedom to end users, but it still has much to learn about transparency and inclusiveness' (Paul 2008).

It is generally the case that, in Battelle's words, 'we're willing to trade some of our privacy – so far, anyway – for convenience, service, and power' (Battelle 2005, 12). We still choose to participate even when we know the score. However, new media has created a new set of issues for audiences and producers to navigate – in terms of how the media exists within our lives and what it enables or closes off. Matters of trust, ethics and control complicate the empowerment we experience in user-generated sites or search.

In October 2007, a BBC program, *Watchdog*, set out to demonstrate the risk of social networking media by creating a fake Facebook user and asking 100 people to become their friend. Thirty-five people accepted the request and at least one gave the BBC enough information to open an online bank account and apply for a credit card in their name. There have been instances where users have also expressed resistance to privacy infringements. MoveOn.org conducted a Facebook campaign against one of the social networking site's own features. In less than ten days more than 50,000 Facebook members signed a petition objecting to Beacon, a program designed to send messages to users' friends informing them of e-commerce transactions (and spoiling a few Christmas presents along the way).[5] Facebook now asks for permission before sending purchase

---

5   MoveOn's Facebook group now has over 200,000 members. The group's page can be viewed at: www.facebook.com/group.php?gid=114387775262356

tracking information to its newsfeeds. Whether these concerns are well founded or not they are part of the experience of the new media environment.

How is this different to other media? With broadcast and print media ownership the issues are less personal. Strangely, although the *Watchdog/Facebook* experiment was cited in newspaper reports, none questioned whether the BBC was acting ethically by creating a fake friend for real people – except maybe those it befriended. The ethical concern with broadcast media is that certain types of news and entertainment are given primacy; that we, as audiences, are not told the whole truth. But it is a more distant concern. In response to such fears, media ethnographers have uncovered a complex relationship between audiences and texts. Audiences can know that large media corporations sometimes produce good entertainment or useful information and commentary. They also know that they can tune out, or seek alternative sources, when they mistrust or dislike what's on offer. Audiences rarely take texts as they were intended and read and use media in all kinds of unexpected ways. As Nick Couldry writes, 'the structures of media production and particularly the dynamics of concentration and conglomeration, do not, of themselves, tell us anything about the uses to which media products are put in social life generally' (Couldry 2006, 36). In other words, it is hard to see the causal connection between a media text and our daily lives.

In the online environment our own networks, purchases and personal interests are up for grabs. For social networking media in particular, the causal connection between 'text' and our daily lives can be felt in very direct ways. Making media might feel empowering but it doesn't solve media ethics: whether the media acts in the best interests of society. Online media companies do have the powers of selection (using algorithms and bots rather than an editor's control). But in a media environment characterised by 'information overload', tools that assist us to search and discriminate are not implicitly a bad thing.

Battelle observes that 'as far as the internet ecosystem is concerned, Google is the weather' (Battelle 2005, 183). And the thing about the weather is that it is invisible and often unpredictable. We can anticipate its impact, but we cannot control it. The only visible part of Google is its crazy font. The ways in which Google rates, collates and distributes information remains a trade secret. Maybe they should change their practices and motto to 'Don't Be Confusing'. '

So if there is a role for community media in the online environment it must be to provide explicit alternatives – not just content but also in the way that organisations deal with information and source code. My realisation that community media was becoming lost in a participatory media landscape stemmed from a desire for ethical systems that are clear and recognisable. If we can't see the difference between SYN and MySpace, then how do we make informed decisions about where to post our content?

Media ethics is usually dealt with in industry Codes of Conduct and training manuals for journalists. What's missing is a way to navigate ethical media choices in a system characterised by abundant choice. Nick Couldry argues that journalist training is not enough and poses the following questions:

- What are the ethical standards by which media's own ethical standards should be judged?
- How do those broader ethical standards relate to more general principles for judging how citizens (whether media professionals or not) should behave in relation to media? (Couldry 2006)

His approach to media studies is as a practice-based sociology, asking what people are doing in relation to media across a whole range of situations and contexts (Couldry 2006).

In their book on media ethics, Catharine Lumby and Elspeth Probyn conclude that 'in the end, ethics comes down to use it or lose it. We need to practise ethical reflection, to ask and demand more of the public sphere, and to participate as consumers and producers – or else' (Lumby; Probyn 2003, 10). But *how do we do that?*

Celia Lury, a sociologist at Goldsmiths in the UK, has written that brands are the currency of the contemporary economy because they are a qualitative marker. Where money reduces objects and cultural systems to quantitative measures, brands denote something that is essentially multi-dimensional, adding a more complex form of value. Brands, she tells us, both enable and inhibit relations and they can both reveal and disguise information. A brand asks for an action, or a response, creating an interface between producers and consumers (Lury 2004). Lury's work is interesting because it opens up conversation about how we navigate through media and culture.

Ever since Naomi Klein's *No Logo,* brands have had a bad wrap in the alternative media field (Klein 2000). But if we think about brands as systems that allow us to act and make choices, then brands are important. I suppose I am asking for a return to the consumption end of the equation. We have spent a lot of time thinking about production, 'prod-users' and participation to the point where the broader issues of agency – in relation to the field of available choices – have been lost.

In the end I had to concur with Bryce's initial knee-jerk reaction to MySpace sites. He had wanted to protect the SYN brand – and branding was exactly the issue. Audiences navigate the online world through brands, recognising logos and what companies stand for, but banning MySpace pages was not the answer. Rather, what was needed was a brand to help people make informed decisions when it came to media use and distribution. Why can't we have a 'fair trade' label for media? It works for coffee producers and distributors.

If such a system was introduced a decade ago, it might have impacted on digital radio and television policy too. Spectrum allocation was falling in favour of large commercial companies. Perhaps the government (like Murdoch) assumed that community media was a natural part of the online environment. For SYN, 2007 was the year when the online environment became much more complex than anyone had anticipated.

Incidentally, Paul Culliver did get his Sablotron for Christmas. He was made Online Manager for 2008, despite having just completed his high school certificate and admitting his lack of technical knowledge. He was, however, a very good online editor. And unlike many at SYN, Paul could spell.

Open Source

Clearly, having a dedicated SYN website was necessary. The executive turned their minds and talents to a new syn.org.au website, funded by a substantial grant from VicHealth. 'Each program will be given their own page', said Bryce. 'The producers can upload and control the content shown on that page'. The difference between the new SYN site and MySpace was that, although the website would be visible to everyone, only the SYN membership would carry out content creation and distribution. It was an interesting idea: if it succeeded then the website would strengthen and expand the SYN community and give volunteers even more control over their content. VicHealth was attracted to the notion of healthy forums for young people to participate in. SYN had lots of young people and a good reputation, but the website turned out to be a real problem, although it had nothing to do with online communities or content in the end. Governance and control was the cause.

In May 2006, a company lead by former SYNners was awarded the grant by the Victorian Government (Vic Health) to research the impact of technology and social media on young people's mental health. The company approached SYN to be part of the project, which would mean building a website for the SYN community and monitoring the process over a three year period. It seemed like a good idea; SYN would get a free website and the company would have the opportunity to build an impressive platform to add to its folio.

The process started off well with a great number of SYNners contributing their thoughts and views on what a website for a radio station in the age of MySpace would look like. However, a series of issues surrounding commercial relationships, internal leadership, project management and editorial control (particularly for the user-generated parts of the site) created tension and delays. One of the problems was that the commercial company found SYN's unpaid executive difficult to work with. Many people within SYN had diverging views of how the website should function, what it should look like and what content should be included. SYN leadership of the project changed hands four times, which made it difficult for any one person to own the delicate series of promises and compromises that were made along the way. A series of technical issues surrounding SYN's reliance on RMIT's infrastructure delayed the process and made some elements of the website impossible to deliver.

The disintegration of the partnership was more than a clash of ideas and personalities. There was too much good faith wound into the project. Initially, the idea of former SYN volunteers developing a new website seemed unproblematic. SYNners who were involved in the project at the time were angered by the management style of the commercial company. They felt that the company perceived syn.org.au as their project, rather than SYN's. Both entities continued to try to work together amicably and in late 2008 a completed and functional website was delivered to SYN to launch. However in January 2009 SYN decided to quit the partnership and to build a new website from scratch.

Meanwhile I witnessed the inklings of an alternative approach. A small team of volunteers had set about building an interim site. The online manager, Will Ockenden, made sure it included discussion forums, 'syncasts' (podcasts) and individual pages for programs. Will was completing an IT course at Monash University and had fallen into the role of IT manager by accident. He admitted there were still technical problems that needed resolving, that the functions were 'bolted on', but it was a decent site nevertheless. Will had a personal aversion to Microsoft, so he didn't spend time making the site compatible with Explorer. If you scrolled to the bottom of the site it read: 'This site looks crap in Explorer, get Firefox'.

I had never really associated SYN with the open source movement until that moment. That tiny detail on the interim site intrigued me because the open source movement was based on the idea of a 'public domain' or 'commons' on the internet – just as community broadcasting was a kind of commons on the airwaves. Will preferred Firefox because it is non-proprietary software, or 'free software'. The issue was much bigger than his choice of browser; Will had ethical concerns about how media is made. The 'free' in free software means that the programming code remains visible to all and is therefore freely available, so that others can copy, adapt and share. Richard Stallman, who founded the Free Software Foundation in 1985, came up with a system whereby developers could keep software in the public domain, using a 'copyleft' licence. The movement was intended to counteract the growing trend towards proprietary software and other technical measures that prevented members of the general public from sharing or modifying source code, and therefore from participating in the ongoing innovation and development of the internet (Stallman 2002).

The free and open source software movement (FOSS) has developed its own particular rights discourse. It challenged media and law theorists to think about the architecture of the internet. Of particular concern was the commercial enclosure of a system which was, in its early days, largely driven by collaborative, open 'end user' effort, largely free from any kind of central control. The proliferation and yield of open source development (such as the Linux operating system) was proof that the regime of intellectual property, private control and having information in the hands of a few was not necessarily the most productive economic model. The 'creative commons' was coined – a term to describe a pool of ideas and technologies which we should all have access to. Creators could attach a CC licence to their work, making it free to be copied, adapted and reworked. This primarily legalistic safeguard was intended to ensure that much of the content and code on the net remained free and accessible. But the movement's chief guru, law professor Lawrence Lessig, also argued that freedom and creativity in general would be curtailed if we didn't act immediately: 'Unless we learn something important about the source of that creativity and innovation, and then protect that source, the Internet will be changed' (Lessig 2001, xxii). The online team at SYN agreed. 'Lessig is my hero', declared Ken.

SYN's chief open source programmer was a young man named Tudor Holton. In Ken's words, Tudor is 'a quasi-genius and one of those people who have morals and stick to them'. Both times I met Tudor he was dressed in a suit that he looked too young to be wearing, like a magical, strangely named character caught between two worlds. Or maybe he just stood out at SYN. As an organisation, SYN is nothing like the alternative media groups I had encountered in the past, where media making is driven by ideology or causes. Mostly SYN is full of boys in tight jeans, or geeky school kids – people who are hard to categorise and whose politics is not obviously detected through their lifestyle choices. Tudor, on the other hand, is an anti-materialist vegan. But it is his media ethics, rather than his political beliefs, that make him useful to an organisation like SYN. If SYN needed a software solution and there was none available for free, often Tudor would just write it himself. In 2002 he started working on a new program to provide SYN with a no-cost solution to meet both administrative and programming needs. They called it SYNplayer. It was far from perfect, but it worked and it was free.

Any community radio station in the country could have used SYNplayer, except that it needed some serious testing and an ongoing help team. Ken put in for a grant from the Community Broadcasting Foundation, but the government-derived budget for community media was intended for radio, not code, and SYNplayer only received a fraction of what it needed. Convergence could occur inside organisations like SYN because they had access to IT students and a membership that was generally curious about new media developments. But it would never make it into the more old-fashioned stations without coordination, leadership and sensible resource allocation. Stations were reproducing technologies from scratch at vast expense or paying for commercial licenses. They should have been working with not-for-profit online community media groups to create shared solutions.

For instance, in 2007 a Melbourne-based group called Engage Media launched their open source video-sharing software, Plumi, which has similar capabilities to YouTube. Engage Media are an online community media organisation and are therefore not recognised in policy, do not have the ear of government and receive their funding through disparate agencies and fundraising strategies. Engage Media cannot join the peak body for community media in this country, the Community Broadcasting Association of Australia (CBAA), because they distribute videos online rather than over the air. They find it difficult to source funding for their projects in Australia, largely because Australian philanthropists rarely support websites, despite the fact that the not-for-profit sector as a whole could benefit greatly from their work. Engage Media are a wily bunch and have attracted substantial international interest and funding. That means that their work increasingly takes them out of the country.

I learnt two things about the media through this encounter with SYN's rebel website team. Firstly, the gap between online and broadcast groups must be addressed or the sector risks obscurity. Community media had failed to unite across online and broadcast platforms when it came to important issues such as governance and technologies. As a result, it had become separate from the organisations that it should have been aligning with; groups that sought to give the same media qualities to the web as community media brought to the broadcast era.

SYN is a member of the CBAA, and many SYNners have a close history with the organisation. Three former SYN GMs – Jo Curtin, Bryce Ives and Craig Twitt – have sat on the CBAA board and Georgia Webster became a board member in 2008. At the start of 2009, the CBAA was reviewing its constitution. Georgia started an online discussion asking SYN volunteers if the CBAA should be opened to new members 'who aren't community radio/TV license holders (e.g. non-profit online media groups like vibewire.org)'.

A week passed and no one at SYN commented until the President, Jess Crouch, responded to Georgia's question:

> [The CBAA]... should be down on its knees begging for innovative non-licence holders to join. The fact that clearly no one at SYN cares about this issue (or even knows who the CBAA is) illustrates the image problems that the CBAA has and will increasingly continue to face.

In the online world, not-for-profit and community-based organisations are differentiating their work through open source code, Creative Commons licensing and other measures, both technological and governance related. Meanwhile, the broadcasters are being left behind.

Secondly, there are limits to the creative commons, even for community media organisations. As enthusiasm for the commons was growing within SYN, I suggested they speak to Jessica Coates from Australia's Creative Commons clinic. During that consultation it became clear that copyleft licensing might create administrative burdens for SYN. As Jessica went through some of the issues that they might face, she uncovered some dodgy activities that SYN's management had not even considered illegal until that point. The meeting ended in a somewhat confused and concerned manner. Perhaps SYN was better off not entering into legalistic territory to begin with. Law academic, Kathy Bowrey, summed up the problem: 'It seems to me that this movement, despite its noble intentions as the foundation for a form of freedom, is also a global form of juridification of civil society. It is about securing an identity and consciousness that is expressed as a legal sensibility/subjectivity' (Bowrey 2004). Sometimes it's okay to avoid lawyers, particularly if they are going to make your life more difficult. The property-centred model of creative commons was only one way in which SYN could influence the media ecosystem and it needed to carefully consider whether it was worth it.

Although the public benefits of using Creative Commons made sense to the people present that day, Creative Commons was a narrow means of addressing communication rights. SYN was open in terms of its management structures, governance and through its accessible media distribution platforms. It was a multi-faceted 'open source organisation'.

Leaving SYN

I was in my local coffee shop on a dreary Melbourne morning and spotted Hamish Blake, a leading comedy drive DJ whose show is networked across the country on commercial radio. Hamish and his co-host Andy Lee had a slot on SYN when they were students at Melbourne University. I tapped him on the shoulder, notebook and pen in hand, like a fan after an autograph. I wanted his story.

'You want to ask me about sin? I know all about that,' he said.

'The radio station?'

'Oh yeah, I know all about that too'.

For Hamish, the fact that 'you can jump on air with no experience, and no pressure' was the important thing; 'otherwise a great show might never get a foot in the door'. He and Andy would use SYN to try out new ideas: '99% didn't work – these days we've got that down to about 96%'. And the process?

'I remember early days at SYN, we'd basically meet to drink at the Oxford across the road, get tipsy, do the show, break some headphones and consequently bring SYN closer to being bankrupt'.

So that explains the headphones.

'Great times', he mused.

Meeting Hamish was a reminder that nothing at SYN is permanent. The friends I had there would soon move on. Some might even be the next media stars, but getting there would not be easy. For most SYNners, finding work in the media involved working two jobs, studying and catching the train in from the outer suburbs at dawn to do a show.

I watched the *1700* crew get ready for the live television broadcast in the C31 studios. Two girls were ready on set, looking over notes and checking where the cameras were pointed. A mobile rang only minutes before broadcast and one of the girls answered it. She was already miked up so I could hear her conversation from the switching booth. The caller was a manager from a cinema chain: she was being interviewed for a casual job as an usher. The manager had no idea she was about to be on live television. 'Hobbies? I play basketball… Oh, and I present a television program on C31', she added, almost as an afterthought.

Ever since I had ventured into SYN the issue of work transitions had been in my face. Bryce told me that, from his observations, work experience was one of the primary reasons for getting involved in SYN and that an astounding number of SYNners were achieving their goal. In order to prove the point, he set up an alumni register – a list of the people who were known to have gone on to work in the media industries. He populated it with his friends and other folk he had kept in touch with. Then he asked others to do the same and gradually the list filled out. At the start of 2006 there were 60 people on the list. By the end of 2007 there were around 80, as more moved into paid media work. I decided to track some of them down. With the help of a research assistant I gathered stories from around 30 of the alumni. We found them in the press galleries, producing online media for the ABC, reading television news, writing comedy, running festivals, and even taking chances in entrepreneurial endeavours, such as mobile phone content development. In a kind of informal exchange program, a substantial number of them were working in regional commercial radio while the country kids (Bryce, Craig and Georgia Webster) were running SYN.

By talking to the alumni I hoped to find out whether SYN had really been a significant factor in them getting work in the creative industries. I figured that many would have been studying at the time, probably journalism or a hands-on media degree, and maybe that was a bigger factor. It was difficult to know exactly what worked at SYN when I was inside the whole messy business of it. The interviews surprised me.

When the station was just getting on its feet, only a couple of years back, today's 'alumni' were the people who were in there, making shows, deciding how things would be done and hanging out. 'Imagine in five years time when we're all out of here and we're all employed' they would say to each other. A young woman working at a commercial radio station in Ballarat told me that there were half a dozen SYN people in that town and a few sitting in the same office as her. I was astonished to hear that four out of five of the ABC's Victorian rural radio reporters at that time were former SYNners. One of them, Nikolai, never studied journalism and had produced music programs at SYN, not news. Although it was overstating it, I had to nod when one of the alumni said: 'The whole reason there are people in the media now and they are skilled and trained is because SYN was there'.

I was told some extraordinary stories. A 22-year-old television comedy writer literally got picked off the air. A TV producer was sitting in his car while his wife was doing the shopping. Flicking through the dial, he came across a SYN program and found himself laughing. He tuned in the next week and the week after that and found it consistently funny. The kid was hired. I asked him what he learnt at SYN and he replied 'to not be lazy, because it is such a great opportunity and you don't want to waste it'. He appreciated the importance of preparation, the 'discipline' of making content and having an incentive to focus on his creative work. SYN helped him know what was funny and how to research: 'You learnt everything that you would learn at another radio station except that there was no way you could get involved in another radio station'. Most of them spoke with the same level of conviction. SYN had changed their lives.

In February 2007, *The Age* broke a story about the eldest son of the Treasurer at the time, Peter Costello. Seb (age 20) was about to host SYN's Breakfast program, *Get Cereal*, getting up at dawn for five days a week. The journalist, Daniel Ziffer (a SYN alumni himself) described Seb as 'hyperconfident and frequently hilarious'. Seb claimed to have 'the greatest show since Marconi invented the radio-thingy' (Ziffer 2007). Other papers picked up the story. Seb, who had kept quiet about his famous family to everyone at SYN, became something of a poster boy for the station. As his dad contemplated a career change, Seb's future looked pretty secure. He became a DJ at a regional commercial radio station and is now a producer at commercial talk radio station, 3AW.

Joanna McCarthy studied Journalism and Law at university, helped write SYN's licence application and became SYN's first

President. She worked as a policy officer for the Community Broadcasting Association of Australia before deciding to pursue a more hands-on media career. In 2006, Jo took a job reporting and producing for the Asia Pacific program at Radio Australia and within a year had won the inaugural Department of Foreign Affairs and Trade Elizabeth O'Neil Media Journalism Award.

Anthony Simpson and Anthony Toohey – or 'Ant and Becks' – met at SYN in its earlier years, around the time when popular commercial radio presenters like Hamish and Andy, Ryan Shelton and Jo Stanley were SYN volunteers. The duo were hosting a drive show on a regional station when they were picked up by a programmer from the Australian Radio Network, which operates MIX and Classic Hits stations in capital cities across Australia. Ant and Becks – the 'new kids on the block' – started hosting the drive show on Mix 106.5 in Sydney and Mix 101.1 in Melbourne in January 2010 (Javes 2009).

There were many who knew they wanted to work in the media and were enrolled in a journalism or media studies higher degree when they came into SYN. They sought practical experience and wanted to get an advantage in a competitive job market. In their minds, formal education alone was not enough to secure work. As one said, 'I remember my first lecture [in a journalism degree course] and the lecturer getting up and saying "so many people want to be journalists and there's so few jobs and you're never going to get anywhere" and just walking out feeling so deflated and defeated'. A student who missed out on a place in a journalism course found herself 'faking being a [public relations] student... and sort of freaked out and went "what do I do?"'

Not all of those who ended up working in the media set out with that intention. A former aspiring fashion designer ended up working at triple j, the national ABC youth radio station. One SYNner had wanted to be a teacher at the time; another was studying to be a paramedic. The paramedic student ended up with a $13,000 debt from a degree that is no longer relevant to his career. 'What I got from SYN I couldn't have got from a media degree at Melbourne Uni,' he said. 'It would have been ten times better than a course. And as far as I'm aware industry experience counts for a lot more than a piece of paper. I've got no degree, no professional training but I'm producing a breakfast show for probably the biggest network in Australia'.

A quarter of those we spoke to came into SYN with no media career intentions, not expecting that it would lead them into work. The studios would be subdued at the beginning of a programming grid – just a lone DJ playing music. As the weeks went by, programmers would invite their friends in, ending up with 'whole army of eight special correspondents popping in and out with their little segments and hanging out to do the show'. A young man whose father worked in radio had decided to steer clear of SYN, not wanting to follow in his footsteps. When a friend asked him to fill-in for him on a SYN program he realised 'I actually like this'. Three months later he was working at a major commercial radio network.

Then there was the social alienation of leaving school. Someone mentioned feeling 'cut-off' from friends who had gone to university when 'that wasn't what I was doing'. Hooking up (in the dating sense) was also an incentive for some. A young woman made a chart of everyone she knew at SYN. She categorised them into 'serious relationships, one night stands, that-one-liked-that-one-but-they-never-got-together, and all that kind of stuff'. According to her sample, a lot more than 50% of people at SYN had 'hooked up'.

For this group, social lives and media participation are an easy fit. That blend of lifestyle choices and industry development has caught the attention of cultural policy makers. The growing creative sector is now seen as an integral part of post-industrial economies – essentially a means to jobs and a better GDP. Characterised as the 'creative industries', this knowledge economy spin-off is less concerned with the unique and transcendent aspects of culture and the arts, than the economic outcomes of creative pursuit. But it cannot be seriously investigated or supported without taking into account the intangible factors that motivate its labour force, as well as the currency (content) that it deals in. For instance, training and recruitment at SYN rely on social networks and occur because there is a cultural status attributed to media making. Formal training measures alone would not produce the same outcomes. It is not an easy area to map or grow. One consequence is that cultural theorists and economists have been raiding each other's intellectual closets in an effort to describe trends and shifts. The mirrors to our identity and social complexity have become an issue of national prosperity, resulting, some would say, in the bizarre academic fashion called 'creative industries research'.

Added to that, labour trends generally are changing. In her book *Adult Themes*, Kate Crawford, an Associate Professor at the University of New South Wales, writes that the traditional roles of childhood and adulthood are all mixed up and that education, work and recreation are no longer tied to specific age groups (Crawford 2006). The sociologist's 'standard biography' has us all moving in a linear progression from childhood to adulthood to old age: 'Education is associated with the stage of childhood, work with adulthood, and retirement with old age. But this standard edition has seen some substantial revisions in the last fifty years' (47). Australians now undergo 'life-long learning', work to get through university and delay financial commitment.

SYN similarly made me reconsider what it means to be young right now and (overtly) challenged my assumptions around age, work and education. The organisation is achieving 'graduate' outcomes that many media schools would be envious of, but its success is due to the fact that it exists in the real media environment, with distinct industry qualities and boundaries. To get educated in the media, the SYNners I met had to go outside of their school or university environment and take on unpaid work. The labour transitions they will face are not straightforward and the industry is in a state of flux and confusion. Retirement from SYN occurs at 26.

As Crawford points out, the characterisation of Generation Y as 'kidults' or 'adultescence' disguise broader anxieties about how work practices are changing (Crawford 2006). Teens have the highest rates of unemployment. and non-standard employment such as casual, part-time and contract work now accounts for approximately 40% of all jobs. A former SYNner told me that he 'went through probably ten to fifteen – not just jobs but *industries*, to find what I really liked'. He was only 23 when I talked to him and working in marketing at a commercial radio station. 'SYN has given me a career', he stated.

I suspect that SYN's unconventional training system is successful because it encourages responsibility and initiative. The hyped comments of the alumni – their audacious belief in SYN as a life-altering experience – underscored the importance of preparedness rather than any particular skills set. Richard Riley, the US Secretary of Education in Bill Clinton's administration, once said that 'We are preparing our students for jobs that don't exist, using technologies that have not been invented, to solve problems that we haven't even considered yet' (Riley 2006). The technologies at SYN might be crude or out-of-date in comparison to what they will find in the workplace, but that doesn't matter so much when you are learning how to cope with change.

In contrast, doing work experience at commercial media companies sounded pretty mundane. Statements like 'Well I had previously been working and volunteering at Austereo in more of a promotional capacity but they weren't giving me any training or on air experience', were fairly common. A young woman, who is now a newsreader, pointed out that 'volunteering at a commercial station is a very strange concept. And at the time it was really overwhelming because you're like "wow this is how a real radio station works and I'm actually in here getting paid in free movie tickets to sit and answer phones'". In her enthusiasm to be at a 'real' radio station she didn't consider that a commercial media company was avoiding paying her for menial labour. SYN is very bad at answering the phones – perhaps a good indication that people have more interesting things to learn.

At the end of 2007, I surveyed approximately 350 media workers about their qualifications and transition into paid work. My intention was to find out what proportion of them had volunteered in a community media organisation. (As the community media questions were embedded within a larger survey, the participants would not have known that my interest was in their voluntary experience). The sample spanned workers in the commercial, public service and community media sectors. As I suspected, over half of them (53.5%) had been involved in some form of community media – mostly radio, but also TV, print and web. Interestingly, that figure rose to 64.2% of respondents in the Under 30 category, suggesting that community media is becoming an increasingly important training ground. Media workers under 30 were also twice as likely to have a bachelor media degree qualification and to have undertaken other forms of unpaid work experience. Getting a job in the media is no longer a straightforward path from school to work. Over 80% of the total group that had participated in community media said that it was either 'important' or 'vital' for getting paid work in the media industries.

As the media industries struggle with convergence, organisations like SYN may become increasingly important training providers. In August 2007, Fairfax announced that it was going to halve their cadetships to four at *The Age* and four at the *Sydney Morning Herald*. Of those positions, half would be university graduates and half fresh from school. All cadets would be paid the same, regardless of their level of education (although half will have a HECS debt to pay off) (Simons 2007). The cadet cuts were a forewarning of even greater losses. A year later, 500 Fairfax staff lost their jobs. Although 'the future of journalism' doesn't necessarily rest on the future of large media institutions, the normal pathways to media careers are narrowing.

That said, young people don't always choose the obvious pathways. A talented young SYNner was offered one of those rare school-leaver cadetships at *The Age*. He turned it down and decided to enrol in an arts degree instead – carrying, perhaps, that strangely idealistic belief that people should learn about the world before reporting on it. I ran into the former fashion design student at a party and discovered that she had left the rat race of triple j so she could pursue her visual art. The creative industries are not always the most creative pathways, it seems.

There was more leaving to be done. Around the time of their 2007 awards ceremony, Bryce announced that he had been offered a job at the ABC, running their regional youth web program, *Heywire*. It was not the first time he had been headhunted, but this time he chose to go.

Craig stepped up to be the General Manager and Bryce made the announcement to his inner circle: 'Craig is now what I used to be'.

'Yeah, skinny', said Craig.

For a few months Bryce stayed on the Basecamp discussion list and got shot-down whenever he tried to influence the conversation. Many of his posts went unanswered. He came into the office regularly, only to be met with comments such as 'you just can't keep away' and 'haven't you got a real job now?' Everyone still loved Bryce and they were happy to see him at social events, to get him in as a specialist trainer or to MC fundraisers. He still commanded respect, albeit a different kind: Bryce was now part of the established media.

'I haven't seen you in the discussion forums', I emailed him.

'I think I need to stay away for a while', he replied.

The two of us were sitting in a bar some months later, in a laneway off another laneway. Bryce confided that 'the position at SYN was lonely, stressful'. Most of the volunteers didn't understand the work he did or his aspirations for the place. He had been having a hard time with the board too. A succession of bad bookkeepers had disguised SYN's financial position. When the extent of their debt was revealed, the board took it out on management. The three staffers had to raise money quickly. The public story was that voluntary student unionism had destroyed their income base, but that was just a convenient excuse. RMIT University sent a generous sum of money and the Victorian Government fulfilled a pre-election promise of $50,000 a year for four years. The income from the school tours and detention programs increased with Georgia's restructuring of the education programs and a few new sponsors came on board. SYN recovered within six months. Bryce was already gone.

I asked Bryce if he still thought that 'radio is dead'. He told me he never really thought that – he just said it to get the kids thinking. As for *Pecado*, he now thought that axing it might have been a mistake.

Bryce wasn't running away from SYN. He had been steadily building up SYN's profile and knew it was capable of massive expansion. 'If I had managed for another year there was not a chance that someone under 30 could do the role after me', he said. He had reached the point where his own ambitions would inevitably change the nature of SYN. With his typical charming immodesty, Bryce said that it 'would have become so complicated – the partnerships would have been huge'. SYN could have been propelled into a different kind of youth organisation but he didn't actually want that: 'I was happy for the organisation to be how it was. Not many people will understand that. I want it to be a fresh, open eyes journey with something smart about it as well'.

Besides, 'you start establishing bad habits, get too old', he said. He showed me his collection of before and after photos of himself and other SYN staff members. Ironically, the flipside of a successful youth organisation is premature aging. Bryce wanted SYN to stay young a bit longer.

Children of the Creative Class

Dylan Leach produced and presented SYN's football program, *Kicking Behinds*. Dylan was one of the longest serving SYNners. He had come into the organisation at the age of 14. In 2007 he was preparing for his Year 12 exams yet somehow managed to be present at the SYN offices two afternoons a week. He intuitively named me 'The Spy'.

Although only 17 when I first met him, he was a big kid, with a booming voice and a thing for practical jokes. Dylan was also a formidable talent. Football stars were happy to talk to him and he was given a coveted press pass to the MCG. I am not sure if blokes like Sam Chisholm and Kerry Packer will dominate the media in the future, but it struck me that Dylan had the potential to be one of them. SYN, however, discouraged anyone from turning out like that. You had to be a team player, whether you liked it or not, and kids were regularly pulled up on discussion forums if they said anything remotely bullish. The SYNners even made Dylan wear a bear suit at their awards night and hug the winners.

Dylan and his co-star on *Kicking Behinds*, Tim Brown, began their media careers during aftercare at primary school. The *Talking Pointless* newspaper ran from 1998–2002 – Grade 3 to Grade 6. In total they produced 155 issues, entirely by Texta. '*Talking Pointless* was pre-pubescent media at its finest and a total empire within the school', Dylan told me in his mogul-like manner. The paper

went national when *The Chaser* began inserting issues into their
own publication. In 2002, George Negus did a story on *Talking
Pointless* for ABC television.

Dylan lent me a few random issues. Headlines included 'Star
Wars Fever Hits Aftercare!' and 'The 10 Dumbest Homework
Excuses'. The main themes included banks, television programs
and sport, plus a marginal gesture to lifestyle media called 'The
Girls Corner'. The paper came with coupons for 'Beforecare Xtra
Milo' and 'free sleeping bag while you are queing' (sic). *Talking
Pointless* was childish but you couldn't blame them for that.

Bryce had warned me during our first meeting that SYN
attracted 'school captains and tertiaries'. Dylan wasn't either of
those, but he was part of a new kind of elite. He had been brought
up in a household where making media is encouraged (his parents
are well-known media names). Richard Florida, a professor who
heads up a Prosperity institute, has identified an ascending creative
class, consisting of knowledge workers and creative types who use
their talents and technologies to get ahead (Florida 2002). The kids
at SYN – or some of them, anyway – were the children of the
creative class. Digital literacy might not have made it into schools,
but it is becoming a form of class accomplishment in the home, like
piano playing was in Jane Austen's time.

The Salvation Army project – still in development at that point
– was therefore addressing a class issue, albeit a slightly different
one to their usual welfare mandate. SYN and The Salvation
Army would work together to teach homeless and disadvantaged
young people media skills. The project was not exactly unique;
SYN already had partnerships with the Jesuit Social Services and
other youth work agencies, although these were dwindling because
of SYN's lack of social work experience. It was still an under-
researched area. We wanted to test some fairly wild claims: that
media production could transform a life, or maybe intervene in
structural problems such as basic economic need.

The slow development of Youthworx (or YWX, as it became known) was frustrating. At one point my research team speculated whether The Salvation Army had a problem with the fact that these kids identified themselves as 'SYNners'. The researcher who was our liaison with The Salvos started calling the station 'S-Y-N' in their presence. When the project finally got through the cryptic administrative structures of the university and the Church it was up and running with impressive speed.

Reverend Craig Campbell, who was running Brunswick Youth Services (a wing of the Salvation Army) at the time, told us that most of the kids who come through his door live their lives 'in 20 minute segments'. The past is too difficult to reflect on; the future is not something they give much thought to. Many of the SYNners, on the other hand, were making conscious decisions about their future. Perhaps the digital divide is not just about access to technologies (the classic definition of 'digital divide'), but an awareness of how to get by in the uncertain knowledge economy.

My own time at SYN was up, just as the YWX partnership got going. I could see that it was going to be a different story to the one I had witnessed. There were youth workers involved, and adult 'expert' media-makers, and a certain top-down guidance that SYN never had. The studio and training space was located at Brunswick Youth Services, rather than The House of SYN, creating something of a divide between the SYNners and the new kids. The very first YWX group went and paid SYN's $5 membership fee and signed up for training off their own bat. However, they never showed up for training, indicating that YWX would need to do more than simply introduce them to the station. I had expected a difficult marriage between a massive evangelical charity and the unpredictable, 'open source' structure of SYN, but things were working out okay. Maybe it is the nature of the third sector that such organisational differences can be overcome without too much trouble. SYN and salvation are not so far apart after all.

Bringing It Home

Rorie Ryan, the kid who started 3TD radio, enrolled in a university course at RMIT, which he never completed. SBS Radio offered him a job as a technician and he took it. Paul Van Eeden and Colin Thompson stayed at Thornbury High and now dedicate their time to Class TV, broadcasting school-made video content on Melbourne's community TV channel. They have also started a new project, ClassNet,[6] and hope it will encourage more schools to engage in media production and distribution. It's fair to say that Paul and Thommo have done more for media education and digital literacy than any other teachers in the country. In 2007, Paul Van Eeden was awarded Victorian Teacher of Year.

Georgia Fox wrote a reflective piece for the end of year, post *Pecado* e-newsletter:

> Given that the most creative and profound imaginings often arise through personal suffering, SYN would like to recognise the importance of failure; the strengthening power of loss, for it inevitably prompts reflection, rebirth and growth.

She was referring to the dismal performance of the Unisexicorns netball team. They finished on the bottom of the ladder of the lowest grade.

Aside from that, SYN was doing fine. A new kind of transformation was taking place. I had been fully aware that the boys were in charge at SYN; it was reflected in the culture of the organisation and the staffing. Then suddenly it flipped. Jess Crouch was elected as President towards the end of my time there (although not without controversy as she was dating the station manager, Craig, at the time). A new administration manager was employed, Emma Sharp, who had moved to Melbourne from Edge Radio in Hobart some years before. With Georgia

6   www.classnet.com.au

and Emma on staff and Jess as President, the girls were gaining ground.

In early 2008 Jess sent out an email to the SYNners:

> Craig has done so much for SYN – so much so that some people think he actually invented it. There'll be time to sing his praises and give him shit about being born in the 1970s later, but for now, I just wanted to keep everyone in the loop about this. Craig's last day will be Friday 16 May.

They organised a surprise party (easy, as he wasn't on Facebook) and designed Craig facemasks, resulting in a room full of Twitts. One of Craig's reasons for leaving was that he felt too old to be at SYN. He worked as a Grants Administrator at the Community Broadcasting Foundation for nearly two years, before moving to Tanzania to work for an aid organisation in early 2010.

Esther Anatolitis, whose time at Craft Victoria had come to an end, replaced Craig as General Manager, even though she was older. The House of SYN suddenly started to look different. Soft lighting replaced the harsh fluoro. The small meeting room was turned into the GM's office and fitted out with groovy retro furniture and pot plants. The girls were definitely in The House.

I wondered whether *Pecado* would make a comeback with Esther in control, given her experience in print media, but Esther was offered a flash job at an arts festival and took it, having spent only three months at SYN. She had reviewed the organisation's operations and made sure everything was running smoothly. Georgia Webster, by virtue of her age and history at SYN, had a stronger connection with the volunteers anyhow. Georgia was appointed General Manager.

Esther had left, but SYN's experiment with having a highly qualified staff member over-30 was not over.

In late 2008, after Georgia became General Manager, the position of Education and Training Manager fell vacant. For the first time, a staff member was hired who had no previous connection with SYN. Nicole Hurtubise, a Canadian who ran the youth arts program at a local library and was a long-time volunteer at Melbourne community station 3CR, became SYN's Education and Training Manager in late 2008.

Georgia credits the work of former GMs, including Craig Twitt and Esther Anatolitis, in stabilising SYN financially and operationally. With Georgia managing SYN, Emma working as assistant manager and Nicole steering the education and training programs, SYN has matured.

In her first months as manager, Georgia focused on fixing the SYN website. She worked with VicHealth to salvage remaining grant funds for the website after the fraught partnership with the commercial company was severed. The website was put to tender in 2009 and new developers were hired. The site went live on 3 February 2010. Georgia explains that engaging volunteers with the website means that the SYN staff 'can't dictate stuff and can't force. There's got to be an inherent value for volunteers in using the syn.org space'.

Demand for SYN training has increased. SYN trainers are now formally recruited and have to demonstrate a skill as part of their interview. One applicant taught the staff how to speak Polish. Another made mojitos. SYN Info Nights are capped at 40 people, with half of those places reserved for under-18s. At the House, technical mishaps and funding shortages are still the norm, but the phone gets answered a little more often.

In 2010, SYN celebrated the ten-year anniversary of its incorporation. A constellation of former SYNners is sprinkled over the Australian media industry: presenters, producers, reporters, techs, writers and editors working in commercial, government and community media organisations.

The prominent staff, board members and volunteers from the past few years have mostly moved on, though many remain close to

SYN. Jess Crouch ended her term as SYN President in late 2009 and moved to London where she now works for Amazon. Bryce left the ABC for musical theatre but he sits on the SYN board. So does Will Ockenden. Will is a national rural reporter at the ABC – and he still hates Microsoft.

The SYNners are also moving into television.

Dylan Leach was producing a new footy show on Channel 7 called *The Bounce,* which was axed shortly after its debut. He works regular shifts at Melbourne's sports broadcaster, SEN. Nikolai Beilharz now works as a television presenter on *The Rural Quarter* – a short program featuring on ABC's new 24-hour digital news channel, *ABC News24* – while presenting radio for *ABC Rural* in Mildura.

Get Cereal TV was something of a catalyst for television at SYN. Prior to the show's pilot in 2008, there was a divide between radio and television. The expansion of *Get Cereal* into television and the influence of people like *Get Cereal TV*'s creator, Tahlia Azaria, and SYN's current TV Manager, Tim Kennedy, helped many SYN volunteers realise that you didn't have to be radio or television. You could be both.

SYN volunteers are currently producing 11 hours of live television each week and SYN has received funding from the Community Broadcasting Foundation to develop a TV training program. Increasingly, young people rocking up to SYN Info Nights ask about television.

The 2008 community radio ratings revealed a 21% increase in the monthly listenership over two years (McNair 2008). Community broadcasting, it seems, is the only broadcast media with growing audiences. 'Can we now declare that new media is dead?' my colleague Chris Wilson asked me.

While those ratings showed an increase in monthly listenership of community radio, SYN's radio ratings fell. A 2009 survey showed that weekly listenership of SYN had dropped from

124,000 to 80,000 in people aged 15 and over (McNair 2009). SYN emphasised that these results show the station is reaching listeners where it counts. The SYN website reads:

> Our target audience is 12–25 year olds, and this survey shows we're hitting the mark – only 18% of all Melburnians fit in that grouping, yet 54% of the SYN audience are in that age bracket. We're well skewed to the culture, ideas and perspectives of younger listeners. (SYN Media 2010)

Not all of the youth radio licensees survived. The regulator, ACMA, declared that Groove FM – a Perth-based licensee – did not perform 'at the level and with the outcomes expected of community broadcasters'. Following a few warnings, ACMA decided not to renew Groove's community radio licence. ACMA's assessment was that the station lacked management expertise, failed to serve the youth community of Perth and that its' programming was too 'narrow' (ACMA 2008). In a move reminiscent of the Hitz FM days, Groove maintained that it was kicked off the air because it was a threat to the commercial stations. Bryce liaised with Groove on behalf of the CBAA during the review process. He thought ACMA's assessment was correct: Groove was not providing the level of access and participation that was required of a community broadcaster.

Despite the positive radio ratings, the fate of this large, odd sector of the media was looking uncertain. Some parts were falling off, or going in their own direction. The Christian broadcasters had been doing their own thing for some time. A number of regional radio stations and all of the television stations except Melbourne were defecting from the CBAA, carrying out their own lobbying. The Labor Government was holding back on digital broadcasting. Then Access 31, Perth's community television channel, went insolvent. Indigenous Community Television, a satellite service for remote audiences, was kicked off the satellite channel it had been using.

'I worry that it could be the end', Bryce said at our last meeting.

SYN is now broadcasting digitally, but Georgia Webster says that for the time being SYN is happy, initially, to simulcast its analogue broadcast. For the forseeable future, spectrum allocation will limit what SYN can do with digital, but the arrival of digital radio presents a host of new challenges for the community broadcasting sector.

In the CBAA's response to ACMA's Digital Dividend Green Paper, the peak body calls for parity with the commercial and government broadcasting sectors, arguing that as additional spectrum becomes available over time, there should be 'a process to prioritise community broadcasting licensee entitlements' (CBAA 2010, 9).

There is the need for equipment and infrastructure that affords regional, rural and remote broadcasters the capacity for digital transmission. Then for metropolitan stations like SYN – one of a handful with a sliver of spectrum for digital-only services – resourcing becomes an issue.

How will SYN accommodate an additional radio service with one production studio? Will the station have the volunteers to sustain a digital-only service and if so, what forms will that digital channel take? Will it be an all-access based service with a handful of flagships like SYN's existing analogue broadcast?

Commercial broadcasters have used their digital spectrum for varied purposes, though in many cases, not for varied content. Recently, ACMA exempted commercial digital radio stations from local music quotas until 2013. ACMA Chairman Chris Chapman stated that the exemption would allow broadcasters to 'experiment with programming formats' and gave examples of 'niche services such as 'event channels' like Pink Radio and Radio Gaga' (ACMA 2010). Both were Austereo digital stations that played non-stop Pink and Lady Gaga when the artists toured Australia. Local labels and independent music associations snorted at the suggestion that

Pink and Lady Gaga were what passed for niche content in the digital radio era.

In mid-2010 Austereo launched U20 – a digital youth radio station for those aged 20 and under. U20's website is bright and enthusiastic, calling the station 'radio built by you… you don't need a recording studio, just a computer and a microphone'. There are catches. One SYNner who looked into U20 says that you pick whatever music you like, so long as it's from a list of music handpicked for U20 presenters. Conceptually, the station shows that DIY has gone mainstream, and what's left is to distinguish genuine forms of participation from publicity stunts.

To me, it was all part of the same problem. Confusion over what community media meant in the online environment was spilling into policy arenas. The old battles over access to spectrum, licences and communication rights had made community media a distinct part of the broadcasting environment, albeit one that was subordinate within a mass media model. Now that the media as a whole had become more participatory, community media was looking lost. The online environment had produced its own communication rights movement – in the form of the open source and creative commons movements – but it was mostly the domain of techies and lawyers. The online groups were off doing their own thing while the broadcasters were beginning to look outdated and redundant.

Nonetheless, my time inside SYN led me to conclude that the community, not-for-profit media sector does have the potential to play a big part in the new media landscape. In the past it has been marginal in comparison to mainstream media. Now it has the capacity to provide structure, governance and ethical systems in a media environment characterised by abundance, participation and 'information overload'.

Digital literacy will most likely be one of its core functions. Although schools will hopefully catch up, the real work will come from the media itself – the places where the languages, forms and colloquialisms of a digitally literate society are created. Organisations like SYN will transmit those developments back into the education system. They will continue to teach the teachers.

The SYNners also have another important role to play. As Gen Y, they know the value of image, of branding, of consumption and self-promotion – all of those things that community media was supposed to stand against. With that understanding, SYN might still manage to drag a complex and divided sector out into a different kind of media world and make it visible. I could see that a new system of media ethics was being built – ethics in the form of consumer choice and producer participation. New media ethics is not about telling people what they can and can't do (SYN knows that better than most). But you can build awareness and get people involved – on a larger scale than ever before.

I said at the start of this book that SYN was a character. By the time I left I had gotten to know her well (SYN started as a boy but became a girl). SYN is a good citizen; ready to share her knowledge with other groups. She has run away from home and lives in a student share house where she is doing just fine. In that house there are squabbles over who left the door unlocked. She decorates the house with found objects and tries not to electrocute herself while fixing appliances. SYN is open minded – caring little for formal politics but concerned about the important stuff, like the future of the planet. She is smart – although she swears too much – but most importantly, SYN has a 'licence to make things happen' and she knows it.

Acknowledgements

Thanks to everyone at SYN Media (past and present), Open Spectrum Australia, C31 and the CBAA. It's not easy writing about friends, so I hope this book is read in the spirit in which it was intended – with fun and affection. I admire you all immensely.

Thanks also to my co-researchers on the Youthworx project: Denise Meredyth, Julian Thomas, David Mackenzie, Aneta Podkalicka, Jon Staley and Chris Wilson. I have left the sequel (Life of YWX?) for you guys and I know it will be fabulous.

A number of research assistants contributed to this project. Firstly, very big thanks to Mary Kozlovski for updating this book after it had been sitting on the sidelines for a while. Ligia Yap, Robin Mitchell and Chris Wilson also helped me collate online data as well as conduct interviews, focus groups and surveys. I have worked hard to disguise the hard data (for the sake of story), but you all made this a much better book. And a very big thanks to Nathan Hollier at Monash University Publishing.

An excerpt from this book was published in *Griffith Review*, Edition 24, May 2009.

Bibliography

Australian Associated Press. 2010. 'GetUp has another court victory'. *The Age*. Released online 13 August 2010. Accessed 6 September 2010. Available from: http://news.theage.com.au/breaking-news-national/getup-has-another-court-victory-20100813-122t3.html

Australian Communications and Media Authority. 2010. 'ACMA media release 83/2010 – 1 July'. Australian Government. Released online 1 July 2010. Accessed 13 August 2010. Available from: http://www.acma.gov.au/WEB/STANDARD/1001/pc=PC_312202

Australian Communications and Media Authority. 2008. 'ACMA media release 15/2008 – 22 February'. Australian Government. Released online 22 February 2008. Accessed 1 March 2008. Available from: http://www.acma.gov.au/WEB/STANDARD/1001/pc=PC_310981

Battelle, J. 2005. *The Search: How Google and Its Rivals Rewrote the Rules of Business and Transformed Our Culture.* New York: Portfolio.

Beecher, E. 2007. 'War of the words: the future of journalism as a public trust'. *The Monthly* (June 2007): 22-26.

Benkler, Y. 2006. *The Wealth of Networks: How Social Production Transforms Market and Freedom.* New Haven, Connecticut: Yale University Press.

Bentley, T. 2007. Email interview with [the author]: Melbourne.

Bentley, T. 1998. *Learning Beyond the Classroom: Education for a Changing World.* London; New York: Routledge.

Bowrey, K. 2004. 'The new, the bad, the hot, the fad – popular music, technology and the culture of freedom'. Presented at the Annual Conference on New Directions in Copyright. 29–30 June; AHRB Copyright Research Network, University of London.

Buckingham, D. 2000. *After the Death of Childhood.* Malden, Massachusetts: Polity Press.

Community Broadcasting Association of Australia. 2010. 'Broadcast and spectrum planning issues related to Digital Dividend Green Paper'. Response to Digital Dividend Green Paper: Submission by the Community Broadcasting Association of Australia. Accessed 11 August 2010. Available from: http://www.cbaa.org.au/sites/default/files/Digital_Dividend_CBAA_Submission_Final.pdf

Chalke, D. 2007. Interviewed on 'Connection breakthrough or breakdown?'. *Difference of Opinion,* Australian Broadcasting Corporation. Released online 23 April 2007. Available from: http://www.abc.net.au/tv/differenceofopinion/content/2007/s1904089.htm

Couldry, N. 2006. *Listening Beyond the Echoes: Media, Ethics and Agency in an Uncertain World.* Boulder, Colorado: Paradigm.

Crawford, K. 2006. *Adult Themes: Rewriting the Rules of Adulthood*. Sydney: Pan Macmillan.

Crouch, J. Quoted in 'Comments, corrections, clarifications and c*ckups'. *Crikey*. Released online 23 April 2008. Available from: http://www.crikey.com.au/2008/04/23/comments-corrections-clarifications-and-cckups/

Daley, E. 2003. 'Expanding the concept of literacy'. *Educause Review 38* (2) (March/April): 32–40.

Davis, M. 1997. *Gangland: Cultural Elites and the New Generationalism*. St. Leonards, New South Wales: Allen & Unwin.

Dee, G. 2007. Interview with [the author]: Melbourne.

Digital Radio Plus. 2010. 'Digital Radio Industry Report 2010'. *Digital Radio Plus*

Doherty, B. 2007. 'Labor battles against new voting roll law'. *The Age*. Released online 17 May 2007. [access 17 May 2007]. Available from: http://www.theage.com.au/news/national/labor-battles-new-voting-law/2007/05/16/1178995236253.html?page=fullpage

Eltham, B. 2009. 'The curious significance of triple j'. *Meanjin* 68 (3): 52–58.

Eltham, B. 2007. 'The young voter theory'. *New Matilda*. Released online 19 November 2007. Accessed 19 November 2007. Available from: http://newmatilda.com/copthis/?p=141

Ferraro, C. 2007. 'School jocks on air'. *The Age*. Released online 8 October 2007. Accessed 8 October 2007. Available from: http://www.theage.com.au/news/tv--radio/school-jocks-on-air/2007/10/07/1191695737306.html

Florida, R. 2002. *The Rise of the Creative Class: and How It's Transforming Work, Leisure, Community and Everyday Life*. New York: Basic Books.

Goodman, S. 2003. *Teaching Youth Media: a Critical Guide to Literacy, Video Production and Social Change*. New York: Teachers College Press.

Harrison, D; Arup, T. 2010. 'GetUp! High Court win overturns Howard's electoral laws'. *The Age*. Released online 6 August 2010. Accessed 20 August 2010. Available from: http://www.theage.com.au/federal-election/getup-high-court-win-overturns-howards-electoral-laws-20100806-11m31.html

Hartley, J. 2008. 'Repurposing Literacy: The Uses of Richard Hoggart for Creative Education'. In Owen, Sue (ed). *Richard Hoggart and Cultural Studies*. Basingstoke: Palgrave.

Havelock, E A. 1988. *The Muse Learns to Write: Reflections on Orality and Literacy from Antiquity to the Presence*. New Haven: Yale University Press.

Holme, R. 2004. *Literacy: An Introduction*. Edinburgh: Edinburgh University Press.

Hopkins, N. 2006. 'Murdoch pushes for competition across spectrum'. *The Australian*. 29 June 2006.

Hunter, I. 1994. *Rethinking the school: subjectivity, bureaucracy, criticism.* St Leonards: Allen & Unwin.

Huntley, R. 2008. 'Exit right: the unravelling of John Howard [Correspondence]'. *Quarterly Essay 29*. Melbourne: Black Inc.: 103–106.

Jackman, S; Brent, P. 2007. 'Rolls close, young voters still underrepresented'. *Republished from Crikey*. Released online 29 October 2007. [access 29 October 2007]. Available from: http://mumble.com.au/misc/20071029_crikey_electoralroll.htm or http://www.crikey.com.au/Election-2007/20071029-Young-voters-still-under-represented-on-the-electoral-roll.html

Javes, S. 2009. 'Off the bench, into the fray'. *The Age*. Released online 2 November 2009. Accessed 20 August 2010. Available from: http://www.smh.com.au/new/entertainment/tv-radio/off-the-bench-into-the-fray/2009/10/31/1256835186203.html

Jenkins, H. 2006. *Convergence Culture: Where Old and New Media Collide.* New York: New York University Press.

Klein, N. *2000. No Logo: Taking Aim at the Brand Bullies.* Toronto: Knopf Canada.

Layton, C. 2008. 'Bridging the abyss: why a lot of newspapers aren't going to survive'. *American Journalism Review* (June/July 2008). Accessed 2 August 2008. Available from: http://www.ajr.org/article.asp?id=4517

Lessig, L. 2001. *The Future of Ideas: The Fate of the Commons in a Connected World.* New York: Random House.

Letch, K. Interview with [the author], 16 July 2010: Melbourne.

Livingston, S. 2009. *Children and the Internet: Great expectations, changing realities.* Cambridge: Polity.

Lonely Planet. 2011. *Lonely Planet's Best in Travel 2011: The Best Trends, Destinations, Journeys & Experiences for the Upcoming Year.* Footscray, Vic.: Lonely Planet, 2010. Excerpt in 'World's top ten cities for 2011 named', *WAtoday.com.au.* Accessed Nov 4 2010. Available from: http://www.watoday.com.au/travel/traveller-tips/worlds-top-10-cities-for-2011-named-20101104-17fc8.html?autostart=1.

Lumby, C; Probyn, E. 2003. *Remote Control: New Media, New Ethics.* Cambridge: Cambridge University Press.

Lury, C. 2004. *Brands: The Logos of the Global Economy.* New York: Routledge.

Marr, D. 2007. 'His Master's Voice: The Corruption of Public Debate under Howard'. *Quarterly Essay 26*. Melbourne: Black Inc.

McDonnell, K. 2006. *Honey, We Lost the Kids: Re-Thinking Childhood in the Multimedia Age.* Melbourne: Pluto Press.

McNair Ingenuity Research. 2009. *'Listening to SYN 90.7 FM Melbourne: April/May 2009'.* Prepared for SYN 90.7 FM Melbourne. New South Wales: McNair Ingenuity Research.

McNair Ingenuity Research. 2008. *'Community radio national listener survey: summary report of findings'.* Prepared for Community Broadcasting Association of Australia. New South Wales: McNair Ingenuity Research. Released online 3 November 2008. Available from: http://www.cbonline. org.au/media/McNairListners2008/FullNationalListenerSurvey2008.pdf

Meadows, M; Forde, S; Ewart, J; Foxwell; K. 2007. 'Community media matters: An audience study of the Australian community broadcasting sector'. Brisbane: Griffith University.

Megalogenis, G. 2007. 'Gen Y registers Kevin's really on a roll'. *The Australian.* Released online 27 October 2007. Available from: http://blogs. theaustralian.news.com.au/meganomics/index.php/theaustralian/ comments/gen_y_registers_kevins_really_on_a_roll/desc/P75/

Mitch, D. 1992. *The Rise of Popular Literacy in Victorian England: The Influence of Private Choice and Public Policy.* Philadelphia: University of Pennsylvania Press.

Montgomery, K C. 2007. *Generation Digital: Politics, Commerce and Childhood in the Age of the Internet.* Cambridge, Massachusetts: MIT Press.

Orr, G. 2010a. 'Voting rights: round two to GetUp!'. *Inside Story.* Released online 13 August 2010. Accessed 6 September 2010. Available from: http://inside.org.au/voting-rights-round-two-to-getup/

Orr, G. 2010b. 'Court by surprise: the High Court upholds voting rights'. *Inside Story.* Released online 6 August 2010. Accessed 6 September 2010. Available from: http://inside.org.au/court-by-surprise-the-high-court-upholds-voting-rights/

Paul, R. 2008. Quoted in 'Ars on Google at 10 years old'. *Ars Technica.* Released online 7 September 2008. [1 October 2008]. Available from: http://arstechnica.com/open-source/news/2008/09/ars-on-google-at-10-years-old.ars

Pew Research Center. 2010. 'The state of the news media 2010: an annual report on American journalism'. Pew Research Center's Project For Excellence in Journalism. Released online 15 March 2010. Accessed 20 August 2010. Available from: http://www.stateofthemedia.org/2010

Powers, W. 2006. 'Hamlet's Blackberry: why paper is eternal'. Joan Shorenstein Center on the Press, Politics and Public Policy Discussion Paper No. D-39. John F. Kennedy School of Government, Harvard University.

Reiss, S. 2006. 'His Space'. *Wired.* Released online July 2006. Accessed 10 August 2007. Available from: http://www.wired.com/wired/archive/14.07/murdoch.html

Riley, R. 2006. Quoted in Westwell, Martin. 'Meeting the needs of an uncertain future'. *Education Quarterly Australia* (Autumn 2008). Accessed 6 July 2008. Available from: http://www.eqa.edu.au/site/meetingtheneedsof.html

Simons, M. 2007. 'Fairfax betrays journalism education'. *Crikey*. Released online 29 August 2007. Accessed 29 August 2007. Available from: http://www.crikey.com.au/2007/08/29/fairfax-betrays-journalism-education/

Smiles, S. 2007. 'Rise in enrolled youth'. *The Age*. Released online 27 October 2007. Accessed 27 October 2007. Available from: http://www.theage.com.au/news/federalelection2007news/rise-in-enrolled-youth/2007/10/26/1192941340876.html

Stallman, R. 2002. *Free Software, Free Society: Selected essays of Richard M. Stallman,* edited by Gay, Joshua. Boston, Massachusetts: GNU Press, Free Software Foundation.

SYN Media. 2010. 'Our audiences'. Accessed 4 August 2010. Available from http://syn.org.au/audiences

Tunn, M. 2007. 'The trouble with Triple j'. *Crikey*. Released online 31 July 2007. Accessed 25 July 2010. Available from: http://www.crikey.com.au/2007/07/31/the-trouble-with-triple-j/

Vincent, D. 2000. *The Rise of Mass Literacy: Reading and Writing in Modern Europe.* Cambridge: Polity Press.

Wilson, J. 2008. 'Will newspapers be first against the wall?'. *New Matilda.* Released online 13 May 2008. Accessed 13 May 2008. Available from: http://www.newmatilda.com.au/2008/05/13/when-revolution-comes

Ziffer, D. 2007. 'Costello the younger takes a crack at public life'. *The Age.* Released online 21 February 2007. Accessed 21 February 2007. Available from: http://www.theage.com.au/news/entertainment/costello-the-younger-takes-a-crack-at-public-life/2007/02/20/1171733764462.html

About the Author

Ellie Rennie is an expert on community and Indigenous media, convergence, communications policy and the creative industries. Her work is well-known internationally and she has delivered keynote addresses at home and abroad. She is currently a Research Fellow at the Institute for Social Research, Swinburne University of Technology. Her work program includes 'The Reinvention of Indigenous Television', funded through the Australian Research Council. Ellie is author of Community Media: A Global Introduction (Rowman & Littlefield, 2006) and writes regular DVD reviews and articles for the quality web magazine *Inside Story* (www.inside.org.au). She is involved in a number of industry and community associations, including the International Association of Media and Communication Research, the Wesley College Institute for Innovation in Education, Open Spectrum Australia and OURMedia/NuestrosMedios.